THE
No-Waste
MEAL
PLANNER

How to create your own delicious meal chains that don't waste a single ingredient

BECKY THORN

SPRING HILL

Constable & Robinson Ltd
55–56 Russell Square
London WC1B 4HP
www.constablerobinson.com

First published in the UK by Spring Hill,
an imprint of Constable & Robinson Ltd, 2013

A copy of the British Library Cataloguing in
Publication Data is available from the British Library

ISBN 978-1-908974 09 9

Printed and bound in the UK

1 3 5 7 9 10 8 6 4 2

Contents

The links in the chain

As a working mother, I spend my life juggling, balancing one commitment against another. Making compromises often seems to be the order of the day. But one area where I have always tried to take the fewest shortcuts was when feeding the family. I wanted to cook as much from scratch as possible, using the best-quality ingredients I could afford. I hoped to provide everyone with quick and tasty family meals, but it soon became apparent that I needed 25 hours in the day (at least!) if I was going to do it all. I realised I had to find a way to minimise my effort and maximise the value from the foods I was cooking. There had to be a way.

I started to think about the meals I had been fed as a child that had seemed to have sprung almost fully formed from the fridge. How did my Nan or my Dad do that? They simply used whatever they had – with a big pinch of inventiveness and imagination thrown in. I needed to harness that in some way. If I planned a menu for the week in which the recipes had ingredients in common, it had to be a win-win. I could maximise my time by cooking ahead, perhaps in bigger quantities, and therefore having partially completed meals waiting in the fridge or freezer. Plus I could minimise waste by using any remaining element of a previous meal to create a completely different dish. Perhaps it would be possible to save myself both time and money, and fool the teenagers into the bargain.

That's when I came up with the idea of food chains. Food chains aim to link one meal to the next by way of using up the bits and pieces that might otherwise be simply scraped into the bin or huddle at the bottom of the fridge. There is nothing new in that, I hear you cry. People have been using up their leftovers for years. What makes the food chains approach different?

Let me illustrate one such chain to show you just what I mean, starting with a typical Sunday lunch . . .

> **Roast chicken** → roast a chicken and enjoy a family dinner, then use the chicken carcass to make a chicken stock to use with any leftover meat to make a huge
> **Chicken risotto** → shape the leftover risotto around salami and mozzarella and add passata to make
> **Arancini with tomato sauce** → use the extra tomato sauce and mozzarella to make
> **Pizza Margarita** with fresh pizza bases.

With just a little thought, I could group together recipes that had elements and ingredients in common, making it possible to use up those odds and ends from one dish to start the next. In some cases, by cooking more food on a previous day, I saved myself preparation time on a following day. Either this made a meal swifter for me to put together or freed me up to do more of the things I enjoy, like making my own dough for pizza bases, for example. I had found a one-size solution to all the things that were bothering – and a way to cut down on my need to juggle so furiously.

So I started to work out some more chains to test the theory and the ideas just kept coming.

○ Ginger biscuits to chorizo and potato hash in a four-link chain.

○ Roast duck to strawberry breakfast smoothie in a four-link chain.

○ Roast lamb to a dirty martini in a five-link chain.

○ Beef brisket to egg fried rice in a four-link chain.

○ Poached salmon to chocolate cake in a five-link chain.

○ Boiled gammon to peanut butter and jam pudding in a four-link chain.

○ Turkey kievs to jalapeño peppers in a four-link chain.

Although the chicken chain follows along a theme, you can see from these examples that is not always the case. They may not even track along sweet or savoury lines; some take some quite surprising turns. Have a look at them and see what you think.

Of course, in a busy household, no system ever works perfectly all the time. But I even managed to put a positive spin on those times when you have no choice but to break the chain!

Have you ever considered what to do with all those plastic take-away boxes that seem to multiply in the cupboard under your sink? Writers of articles published in glossy home makeover magazines would suggest you cover the lid with a floral fabric swatch and fill them with colour co-ordinated buttons (as if!). I, however, have better idea of what to do if you don't want to eat arancini the day after you've had risotto. Just pop the extras in a plastic box, label and freeze it, ready and waiting for the chain to be started up at a later date.

Food chains won't show you how to make a pound of mince feed twelve or even how five loaves and two fishes could get the party started: there are other books for that. But it will help you you get every scrap of value from the goods you buy, reduce waste without compromising on taste, maximise your time and minimise your stress. That's got to be worth a try!

Storecupboard essentials

The way a storecupboard works is very simple. The last thing you want to do is to clog up your cupboards with things you don't need. But if you keep a carefully personalised set of ingredients on hand, you'll always been able to transform your leftovers into something tasty and interesting.

These are the basics that I keep in the cupboard and have assumed you'll have in yours. So when you come to the chains, I've listed everything I expect you already have – listed in alphabetical order so that it is easy to check before you go shopping. Plus I have added everything you need to buy for that particular chain; these are grouped, shopping-list style, into meat, vegetables, and so on. I don't think I need to say that if there's something you don't like or never use, don't buy it (do I?)! And I haven't listed salt and pepper every time – I'll assume you have those.

Baking powder

Bicarbonate of soda

Black peppercorns – for grinding

Breadcrumbs

Brown sauce

Butter

Cake sprinkles – hundreds and thousands etc.

Cardamom pods

Chilli flakes

Chinese five-spice powder

Chocolate – dark

Cinnamon – ground

Cloves

Cocoa powder

Cornflour

Cumin – ground

Eggs

Flour – plain, self-raising and strong bread

Garlic

Gelatine – powder

Ginger – ground

Glucose liquid

Golden syrup

Honey – clear

Horseradish sauce

Jam

Lard or white vegetable fat

Mayonnaise

Milk

Mustard – Dijon, English and wholegrain

Nutmegs – for grating

Oil – olive, sesame and vegetable

Oregano

Paprika – sweet and smoked

Parsley – keep a pot of growing herbs on the window sill

Peas – frozen

Porridge oats

Rice – arborio and basmati

Salt – sea and table

Soy sauce

Dried Apricots

Stock – frozen, chilled, a stock pot or a cube

Sugar – caster, demerara, granulated, icing, soft dark brown and soft light brown

Tabasco sauce

Tahini

Thyme

Tomato ketchup

Tomato purée

Vanilla – pod or extract

Wine – red and white

Wine vinegar – red and white

Worcestershire sauce

Yeast – dried

Za'atar or sumac

Notes and conversions

For beginners, or for others who would like to familiarise themselves with the details of how the book is set out, here are a few notes on how the recipes are presented.

○ The ingredients are listed in the order in which they are used in the recipe.

○ All spoon measures are level unless otherwise stated. 1 tbsp = 15ml; 1 tsp = 5ml.

○ Eggs and vegetables are medium unless otherwise stated.

○ Always wash, peel, core and deseed, if necessary, fresh produce before use and cut into even-sized pieces.

○ Taste the food as you cook and adjust seasoning to suit your own palate.

For quickness, use garlic and ginger purée instead of crushing or grating your own.

All can and packet sizes are approximate as they vary from brand to brand.

Cooking times are approximate and should be used as a guide only. Always check food is piping hot and cooked through before serving.

When the oven or grill is necessary to finish a dish, always preheat it and cook on the shelf just above the centre of the oven (this isn't necessary in a fan oven which heats very quickly and the heat is similar throughout the oven) or 5cm from the heat source for the grill, unless otherwise stated.

Those who prefer Imperial measures can use these conversions (they are approximate for ease of use). If you use American cup measures, a cup is 250ml, or whatever volume fits into the space (so a cup of sugar is 225g whereas a cup of flour is 100g).

Weight

25g	50g	75g	100g	150g	175g	200g	225g	250g	350g	450g
1oz	2oz	3oz	4oz	5oz	6oz	7oz	8oz	9oz	12oz	1lb

Liquid measurements

5ml	15ml	50ml	75ml	120ml	150ml	200ml	250ml	300ml	450ml	600ml
1 tsp	1 tbsp	2fl oz	3fl oz	4fl oz	5fl oz	7fl oz	9fl oz	$^1/_2$pt	$^1/_3$pt	1pt

Oven temperatures

110°C	120°C	140°C	150°C	160°C	180°C	190°C	200°C	220°C	230°C	240°C
225°F	250°F	275°F	300°F	325°F	350°F	375°F	400°F	425°F	450°F	475°F
gas $1/4$	gas $1/2$	gas 1	gas 2	gas 3	gas 4	gas 5	gas 6	gas 7	gas 8	gas 9

Measurements

5cm	10cm	13cm	15cm	18cm	20cm	23cm	25cm	30cm	40cm	45cm
2in	4in	5in	6in	7in	8in	9in	10in	12in	16in	18in

The Meal Chains

Shopping list

1 bunch spring onions

8 floury potatoes for mashing

4-6 large potatoes for frying

20 streaky bacon rashers

100g Caerphilly cheese

150g chocolate chunks

Dried apricots

Raisins

Chutney

From the storecupboard

Brown sauce

Butter

Eggs

Flour - plain and strong white bread

Milk

Mustard - English

Oil - vegetable

Parsley - fresh

Sugar

Yeast - fast-action dried

Breakfast brioche chain

Who doesn't like breakfast? So many choices are on offer – from a double espresso and a flick through the papers to a steaming bowl of porridge topped with fresh fruit compote – there is something for everyone. Call it coincidence or even serendipity but depending on your point of view, something has to be going on in this Breakfast brioche chain.

Bacon and eggs seem to be the theme of this chain. Not always crispy or even runny, they both pop up several times in the following ingredients lists. Bacon and eggs don't appear together in every recipe but they could well accompany each other if you felt the need!

Breakfast brioche → use the breadcrumbs made from the leftover brioche to make →
Glamorgan sausages and mash → use up the additional mashed potato to make →
Potato scones, poached eggs and bacon → use the surplus bacon rashers to make →
Bacon-dusted fries

Breakfast brioche

The only time my teenagers seem to move with any speed first thing in the morning is when they know the bus or train won't wait. Shooting out of the door with a cup of coffee in one hand, they need something sensible to eat. A homemade brioche fills a hole, can be stuffed with a variety of little extras and actually tastes really lovely.

Makes 6 brioche

For the brioche
2 tbsp warm milk
1 x 7g sachet dried yeast
180g strong white bread flour, plus extra for dusting
½ tsp salt
1 tsp caster sugar
2 eggs, beaten
125g butter, very soft but not melted
Oil, for greasing

For the fillings
Chocolate chunks
Raisins
Ready-to-eat dried apricots, chopped
Or what you will

○ In a small bowl or, more likely in my house, an old teacup, mix together the warm milk and yeast. Leave to stand until the yeast has activated and the milk appears to foam.

○ Sift the flour into a large bowl and add the salt and sugar. Make a well in the centre and pour in the beaten eggs. Add the yeast mixture and beat well with a wooden spoon. Keep beating until the very wet dough becomes smooth and less sticky. I usually count one hundred turns of the spoon – well, probably about 125 as I often lose count and have to go back a few numbers just to make sure.

○ Remove the spoon and use your hand to amalgamate the butter into the dough. This is messy but huge fun. Resist answering the phone as the handset gets really sticky if you do.

○ Form into a ball, place in a clean bowl, cover with clingfilm and leave somewhere warm for a couple of hours until doubled in size.

○ Lightly oil a baking tray.

○ Knead the dough again – this is called knocking back the dough – then pinch off lumps of dough and make six cricket ball-sized buns. Place these on the prepared baking tray. Leave them plain or stud with the chocolate, raisins or apricots. Leave to rise again for about 30 minutes.

Save it *These fruity or chocolate brioches won't be any good for the sausages we are making next so you may wish to leave two plain just for that.*

○ Preheat the oven to 180°C/gas 4.

○ Bake for 25–30 minutes until golden.

○ Grab a coffee and run for the bus!

Save it *Any leftover breadcrumbs will go towards the next recipe in the chain. Blitz the leftover brioche in a food processor and use the breadcrumbs within a day or so, or pack, label and freeze for up to 3 months.*

Glamorgan sausages and mash

So quick and easy to make from the staples we all have in the house, I find these a really good standby when someone utters those fateful words, 'Oh, by the way, Mum, two people coming tonight are vegetarians' when you had planned to dump a big tray of nuggets and chips on the table for the ravening hordes about to descend.

Serves 2

For the sausages
125g brioche breadcrumbs
100g Caerphilly cheese, grated or crumbled
40g spring onions, thinly sliced
1 tsp English mustard
1 tsp chopped fresh parsley
1 egg, beaten
1–2 tbsp milk (optional)
A small knob of butter
1 tbsp oil

For the coating
2 tbsp plain flour
Salt and freshly ground black pepper
2 tbsp milk
25 g brioche breadcrumbs

For the mashed potato
8 floury potatoes, peeled and cut into small chunks
A splash of milk or cream
A knob of butter

To serve
Chutney or brown sauce
Peas or other vegetables

Make the sausages

o Place all the ingredients into a large bowl and combine carefully with your hands. If the mixture won't form sausage shapes easily, add a splash of milk until the mixture becomes more pliable.

o Form the mixture into 6 or 8 sausage shapes, then pop into the fridge to firm up.

Cook the potatoes

o Put the potatoes in a saucepan of water, bring to the boil, then boil for 5–10 minutes until soft enough to mash. The tip of a knife should slide into the potato without any resistance. Drain and leave in the pan to steam dry for a minute or so.

Cook the sausages

o Take the sausages from the fridge. Set out the flour, milk and breadcrumbs in shallow bowls and season the flour with salt and pepper. This is an ideal time to enlist child labour. Coat the Glamorgan sausages lightly in flour, then milk and finally breadcrumbs.

o Meanwhile, heat the oil and butter for the sausages in a frying pan.

o Lay the sausages in the hot oil and butter mixture and fry for about 15–20 minutes until golden and crispy, turning occasionally.

Finish the dish

o Mash the potatoes.

Save it *Put aside half the mash before you add the milk or cream and butter.*

---

o Beat the milk or cream and the butter into the mash and season to taste with salt and pepper.

o Serve alongside the Glamorgan sausages with a large dollop of chutney or brown sauce and some vegetables.

Potato scones, poached eggs and bacon

My dad was a fantastic cook. Intuitive and always a little dangerous in his choice of ingredients, he would happily press a tongue, make brawn from half a pig's head, or cook roast beef for 75 at the drop of a hat. It is, however, a much simpler dish that takes me back to time spent in the kitchen with him: potato scones. Using up leftover mash he would quickly mix up these delicious patties, fry them in bacon fat and snaffle them with a shake of Worcestershire sauce before anyone else, apart from me, noticed.

Serves 4

20 streaky bacon rashers
About 600g cold and fairly dry mashed potato
About 150g plain flour (¼ the weight of mash), plus extra for dusting
A pinch of salt
A good knob of butter, melted

To serve
4 poached eggs

Cook the bacon
○ Crispy bacon is best cooked in the oven. Heat the oven to 180°C/gas 4 but don't worry if the oven isn't up to temperature when you put the bacon in.

○ Place the rashers of bacon onto a wire rack and set this over a large baking tray. Pop into the oven and bake for 15–20 minutes until golden brown. The bacon will crisp up on cooling.

> **Save it** *Use about 12 rashers for this and reserve the rest for the bacon-dusted fries. Crispy bacon is very addictive and may get eaten before you have time to make the bacon-dusted fries. Do not let this happen!*

Make the scones

○ Weigh the mash and work out how much flour you will need. Place the cold mash, flour, salt and melted butter in a bowl. Work the ingredients together lightly with your hands until a dough is formed.

○ Take cricket ball-sized pieces of dough and roll them out on a floured surface into rough circles about 7–10mm thick. Cut each circle into four.

○ Heat a griddle or frying pan and add a smear of butter or even some bacon drippings to stop the scones sticking.

○ Fry the scones for 2–3 minutes on each side until browned and crisp.

Finish the dish

○ Serve hot from the griddle with crispy bacon and a runny poached egg.

Save it You can allow the scones to cool and reheat them later in a dry frying pan or griddle for a moment on each side. They also freeze well in a freezer bag, just ready for a lazy Sunday brunch.

Vary it You could use other mashed roots to make similar scones. Sweet potato would certainly work and mashing in some beetroot would surely give a magnificent colour as well as an elusive earthy quality to the scones.

Bacon-dusted fries

There are times when I have been accused of gilding the lily. I would have to agree that there are few ways to improve on a proper chip, lightly salted, doused in vinegar and eaten out of the paper on a cold evening but let me introduce you to bacon dust. Try it and I can guarantee you will wonder how you ever ate chips without it!

Makes about 2 tbsp

5–8 baked crispy bacon rashers
Oil for deep-frying, such as groundnut oil or even beef dripping if being very authentic
4–6 large floury potatoes, peeled and cut into chips

Make the bacon dust

o Crumble the rashers of bacon into a pestle and mortar or into a food processor. A mixing bowl and the end of a rolling pin is a good substitute for a pestle and mortar. Mill the bacon down as finely as possible. You'll have about 2 tbsp.

Save it Use what you need and place the bacon dust into a lidded container. This will keep for a up to a week but this is purely hypothetical as it will vanish as soon as you make it.

Fry the chips

○ Heat the deep-frying oil in a deep, heavy-based pan to 130°C, when it will bubble when you hold a wooden spoon in the oil. Carefully lower the chips into the oil, in a frying basket if you have one, and cook for about 10 minutes until the chips are soft but not coloured at all.

○ Drain on kitchen paper and leave to cool.

Save it *The blanched chips can be kept now for up to 4 hours or so until needed – ideal for snacking or for feeding latecomers.*

Second-fry the chips and serve

○ Heat the oil to 190°C, when a cube of day-old bread will brown in 20 seconds. Return the partly cooked chips to the very hot oil for another few minutes until crispy and golden brown.

○ Drain well and place on kitchen paper to ensure the chips are really dry.

○ Sprinkle liberally with bacon dust to serve.

Cook's tip *Bacon dust will keep for up to 3 days in an airtight box or ziplock bag. Scatter it over buttery corn cobs, use as a topping for salad or try it as a decadent savoury flavouring for popcorn.*

Shopping list

½ cucumber

2 onions

3 spring onions

1kg floury potatoes for mashing

13–15kg belly of pork

750g white fish fillets

250g smoked fish fillets

500ml passata

100g water chestnuts

1 x 50-wrapper pack of wonton wrappers

From the storecupboard

Butter

Chilli flakes

Cloves

Chinese five-spice powder

Eggs

Flour – plain

Garlic cloves

Milk

Mustard – English

Oil

Parsley – fresh

Soy sauce

Sugar – caster and soft light brown

Tabasco sauce

Wine vinegar – white

Crackers and pickles chain

You don't always need to eat a huge meal to feel satisfied. Often a little something will keep you going or perhaps, in my case, feed my greed! The crackers chain has a combination of full-on family meals and tasty titbits to top you up throughout the day.

The tang of vinegar runs through all the dishes in this chain. From the pickled cucumbers to the dipping sauces, the sharp, lip-puckering taste is always in the background, lurking to surprise you.

Crackers and sweet and sour cucumber → use the crushed crackers to make →
Crunchy-topped fish pie with homemade tomato sauce → Keep the remaining homemade ketchup and transform it into the marinade for →
Barbecued slow-roast belly pork → strip the flesh from the cold pork belly and use it to fill →
Barbecued pork wontons

Crackers and sweet and sour cucumber

Lunch these days is taken at the computer, on the hoof and very rarely at the kitchen table. If I can't eat at home, then something homemade is the next best thing. A simple lunch of cheese, crackers and a pile of pickle has kept ploughmen going for centuries so it should be good enough for me. Don't be tempted to use a mandolin to slice the cucumber as the slices will be too thin and the pickling will turn them to mush – believe me, I tried. Also you will keep your fingertips – always useful in the kitchen.

Makes about 40 crackers

For the sweet and sour cucumber
½ cucumber, thinly sliced
½ onion, thinly sliced
2 tsp table salt
50g caster sugar
70ml white wine vinegar
1 tsp chilli flakes

For the crackers
250g plain flour, plus extra for dusting
A pinch of salt
75g butter, straight from the fridge, plus extra for greasing
1 tsp English mustard
75–125ml cold water

Make the cucumbers
○ Put the thinly sliced cucumber and onion into a lidded plastic box. Sprinkle with the salt, stir and leave for about 10 minutes to soften.

○ Whilst this is happening, place the sugar, vinegar and chilli flakes in a small pan and heat until the sugar dissolves. Leave to cool.

○ Rinse the cucumber and onion mixture under cold water, drain and transfer to a bowl. Pour over the chilli and vinegar syrup and leave to steep for an hour or so.

Make the crackers

○ Sift the flour and salt into a bowl. Cut in the cold butter and, using your fingertips, rub the butter into the flour. When the mixture resembles fine breadcrumbs, stir in the mustard. Using a table knife, mix in enough water to form a ball of dough. (This can be done in a processor if you want to faff around washing one up afterwards.)

○ Cover with oiled clingfilm and leave the dough to rest for 20 minutes.

○ Preheat the oven to 180°C/gas 4 and grease a baking sheet.

○ Roll out the dough until about 5mm thick. Cut into shapes of your choice; I use a ravioli cutter and make rectangles but any shape is fine.

○ Place on the prepared baking sheet and prick each one a few times with a fork. Bake for 20 minutes until lightly golden.

○ Transfer to a wire rack to cool.

Save it *Keep any unused crackers in an airtight container until needed, and use them for the next recipe. They will last about five days.*

Finish and serve

○ Find a ploughman to share your lunch of crackers and cucumber. If that fails, how about a colleague instead?

Vary it *There are endless variations to these crackers. Mix in or sprinkle with sesame seeds, Parmesan cheese, poppy or caraway... just use your imagination to make the recipe your own.*

Crunchy-topped fish pie with homemade ketchup

For an island nation, the British eat a tiny quantity of fish. Even then we stick to only a couple of species, batter it, deep-fry it and smother all semblance of flavour with salt and vinegar. I have to admit, though, that the smell of fresh chips wrapped in hot paper parcels is guaranteed to make my stomach growl. It really isn't the best meal to eat regularly so what to do instead? Fish pie is a familiar, yet often surprising dish. The crisply topped duvet of soft potato can hide a magnificent, endlessly changing variety of flavours and textures.

Serves 4

For the ketchup
1 tbsp oil
½ onion, chopped
1 garlic clove
500ml passata
100g soft light brown sugar
100ml white wine vinegar
Salt and freshly ground black pepper

For the filling
4 cloves
1 onion, peeled
750g white fish pieces (cod, haddock, pollack, coley)
250g smoked fish
500ml milk
100g butter
50g plain flour
1 tbsp chopped fresh parsley

For the topping
1kg mashing potatoes, peeled and chopped
70g butter
100g crackers, crushed with a rolling pin

Make the ketchup
○ Heat the oil in a saucepan and fry the onion and garlic for about 5 minutes until softened and translucent.

○ Stir in the passata, sugar, vinegar and season with salt and pepper. Simmer very gently for 20 minutes.

○ Blend with a hand blender or in a liquidiser, then leave to cool before serving.

Save it *This will keep for a week in an airtight container in the fridge.*

Cook the fish

○ Press the cloves into the onion, then place the onion and the fish pieces into a deep frying pan. Cover with the milk and bring slowly to a very gentle simmer. The surface of the milk should barely shiver with excitement. Simmer for 8–10 minutes until the fish just flakes when pushed with a finger.

○ Lift the fish from the poaching liquid. Reserve this liquid but discard the onion and cloves. Break the fish into chunks as you lay it in the bottom of an ovenproof dish.

Make the topping

○ Meanwhile, boil the potatoes in salted water until soft. Drain and place back into the warm pan to steam a little and dry out.

○ Add 50g butter, mash well and leave to one side.

Finish the pie

○ Preheat the oven to 180°C/gas 4.

○ Melt the 100g butter in a saucepan, stir in the flour and cook over a gentle heat for 2–3 minutes, stirring all the time. This prevents that floury, gluey texture that can sometimes afflict white sauces. Little by little, whisk in the milk reserved from poaching the fish. Keep adding the liquid until your sauce coats the back of a spoon. Stir in the parsley and season to taste.

○ Pour the sauce over the fish, dollop on the mash and smooth out a little using a fork.

Improve it *My favourite parts of any potato-topped pie are the crispy bits at the edge. Using a fork to rough up the topping maximises the crisp factor. If you want to pipe the potato, please do, just remember it will make more washing up!*

○ Crumble over the cracker crumbs, dot with the remaining topping butter and bake for 30 minutes until crisp, bubbly and golden brown. Serve with the ketchup.

Slow-roast belly pork with barbecue spices

I know that sometimes people shy away from a cut like pork belly because of the fat content. Butchers are becoming aware of this and are doing their best to provide leaner cuts. Look carefully as you choose the joint and you should be able to buy a piece of belly pork that suits your requirements. Do remember, though, that fat equals flavour and succulence. A little fat under the skin is what makes barbecued belly of pork such a delicious but inexpensive meal.

Serves 4

2 tbsp homemade ketchup
1 tsp English mustard
1 tbsp soy sauce
1 tsp Tabasco sauce
1.3–1.5kg belly of pork
Sea salt and freshly ground black pepper

To serve
Boiled rice
Purple sprouting broccoli or pak choi

○ Preheat the oven to 220°C/gas 7.

○ Mix together the ketchup, mustard, soy sauce and tabasco. Without getting any on the pork rind, brush the meat liberally with this mixture, then place it in a roasting tin. Sprinkle the rind with plenty of sea salt.

○ Slide into the oven and roast for 30 minutes.

○ After 30 minutes, turn the oven down to 160°C/gas 3 and leave to roast slowly for another 3 hours.

Enjoy it *Put your feet up. Organise someone else to hoover, clean and polish.*

○ Take the pork from the oven, cover with foil and leave to rest for at least 15 minutes.

○ Carve the meat into thick slices and serve with boiled rice and steamed purple sprouting broccoli or pak choi.

Save it *Save some of the pork for the next link in the chain.*

Cook's tip *This recipe could easily be replicated with a shoulder of lamb, slow roasted using the same timings. I'd change the marinade a little by replacing the mustard with lemon juice and the tabasco with a crushed clove of garlic.*

Slow-roast pork wontons

Street food has kept the wolf from the door for many travellers: tasty titbits quickly popped into the mouth, savoured and enjoyed – and often for only a few coins. These are, for many, the tastes we recall most vividly from our distant expeditions. Crispy, blisteringly hot wontons instantly transport me to a street corner in Hong Kong. Lit by naked light bulbs strung across a narrow alley, a kerbside kitchen distributed these delicious morsels to a seemingly endless queue of hungry customers. I fell in love with the crunch of the exterior first, then the deep, savoury, umami notes of the interior softness seduced me still further. Oh, the memories . . .

Make sure you only have a few people in your house when you make these. They are very moreish and you won't want to share them with many others.

Serves 4

For the filling
150g slow-roast pork belly, minced or finely chopped
100g water chestnuts, finely chopped
1 tbsp soy sauce
3 spring onions, thinly sliced
1 egg
A pinch of Chinese five-spice powder

To finish and serve
1 pack of 50 wonton wrappers
Oil, for deep-frying
Soy sauce, sweet chilli sauce or ketjap manis for dipping

Ketjap manis is a thick and slightly sweetened soy sauce that you can buy in oriental stores.

○ Combine all the filling ingredients in a large bowl. Give a good stir and leave for a little while to allow the flavours to infuse.

○ Place 1 tsp of the mixture in the centre of a wonton wrapper. Pull the edges up to make a money-bag shape. Pinch together to seal and continue making wontons until all the filling is used up.

○ Heat the oil for deep-frying in a deep saucepan. You want the oil hot but not shimmering. Slowly fry a few wontons at a time for about 3–5 minutes until the wontons are golden. Try not to overcrowd the pan as this will cause the wontons to be soggy.

○ Lift out with a slotted spoon and drain on kitchen paper.

○ Serve with dipping sauces and let the seduction begin.

Shopping list

25 fresh basil leaves (buy a small plant!)

1 celery stick

1 lemon

1kg tomatoes

500g white fish or salmon

284ml double cream

1 loaf of bread

100g day-old bread

200g dark chocolate

2 vodka shots

From the storecupboard

Bicarbonate of soda	Milk
Butter	Oil - vegetable and olive
Cocoa powder	Peas - frozen
Eggs	Sugar - granulated and
Flour - plain	soft light brown
Garlic clove	Tomato ketchup
Golden syrup	Worcestershire sauce

Fish finger sandwiches chain

Bread and cake seem to form the backbone of the fish finger sandwich chain. You really can't go wrong with that now, can you? Fresh bread is a delight and a joy; however, day old bread is one of the most versatile ingredients a frugal cook has in their larder. Try these recipes to discover why.

Fishfinger sandwiches with pea spread → use the remainder of the loaf to make →
Panzanella → use the excess tomatoes from the salad to make →
Bloody Mary sorbet → use up the basil sugar to make →
Chocolate basil cake

Fish finger sandwiches with pea spread

Thankfully there are things we just refuse to grow out of. In our house it's the old student hangover cure, fish finger sandwiches. Here, they have been reinvented and are a far cry from the ketchup-laden doorsteps of our youth, but as a Saturday brunch after just one too many glasses of wine, they still work miracles.

Serves 4

100g day-old bread
Grated zest of a lemon
Sea salt and freshly ground black pepper
1 egg, beaten
500g white fish or salmon, cut into 2 x 8cm strips
Vegetable oil, for greasing
1 loaf of bread or 8 slices

Save it *You'll need the lemon juice tomorrow.*

For the pea spread
200g frozen peas, defrosted
50g butter, softened

To serve
Tomato ketchup (optional)

Make fish finger sandwiches

○ Preheat the oven to 200°C/gas 6 and lightly oil a large baking tray.

○ Take the slices of bread and a box grater or use a food processor and make your breadcrumbs. Better still, ask a child or teen to do this for you; they get to learn a new skill and you can get on with other things. Place the breadcrumbs in a bowl with the lemon zest and salt and pepper to taste.

○ Break the egg into another bowl and beat with a pinch of salt and a little freshly ground black pepper.

○ Take a piece of fish, dip in the egg and then the breadcrumbs. Keep one hand for the egg and one for the breadcrumbs otherwise you end up with digits that resemble fish fingers themselves as they get coated too. Lay the breaded fish fingers onto the baking tray. Bake for 20 minutes.

Make the pea spread

○ Blitz together the peas and the butter using a hand blender or a processor.

Finish the dish

○ Once the fish fingers are cooked, slice the day-old bread thickly. Place a good smear of the pea spread onto half the slices of bread and lay the fish fingers on top. Add some ketchup, if you like. Press the top layer of bread down firmly. Slice in half and indulge. Ketchup is again an optional accompaniment to this most comforting of sandwiches.

Panzanella

I am very fond of tomatoes, garlic, basil and lemons and I'm pretty keen on a slice or two of bread. Combine the ingredients together as panzanella and I'm totally and utterly smitten! My version is slightly different from the classic frugal panzanella in that I crisp the bread in a little oil. I love the mixture of warm crunchy, slightly sweet bread with cool, acidic tomato and lemon. Texture and taste go hand in hand here – try it and you will see.

Serves 4

4 tbsp olive oil
Juice of 1 lemon
1 garlic clove, grated
Several pinches of sea salt
Fresh ground black pepper
1kg tomatoes, diced, reserving the juice
½ loaf uncut bread
Vegetable oil, for frying
A few fresh basil leaves

○ In a roomy bowl, whisk together the olive oil, lemon juice, garlic, salt and pepper.

○ Add 500g of the diced tomatoes, adding as much of the juice as possible. Stir and set aside to allow the favours to meld together.

Save it Use 500g of the tomatoes for today and save 500g for the sorbet. Keep them away from the fridge as it seems to suppress the real tomato flavour somewhat.

○ Cut the bread into thick slices, discard the crusts, and cut or tear the bread into cubes.

○ Heat enough vegetable oil to coat the bottom of a large frying pan, then fry the bread cubes until golden and crispy. Drain on kitchen paper and tumble into a bowl.

○ Quickly pour over the tomato and dressing mix. The bread should almost sigh as you combine the two elements together.

○ Tear some basil over the dish to finish.

○ Sit outside in peace with a large glass of wine and imagine someone else is washing up.

Cook's tip *If you just don't fancy a big bowl of panzanella or you'd rather be a little more dainty, then use the self-same ingredients to make bruschetta. Whisk the dressing ingredients together and slide in the chopped tomatoes. Leave to macerate. Cut the bread into fairly thick slices and rub them over with a garlic clove. Pop the bread on a griddle, if you have one, or a dry frying pan if you don't, and allow to get a little colour and warm through. Place on a plate, spoon over the tomatoes and scatter with torn basil and a drizzle of olive oil.*

Bloody Mary sorbet

Cocktails can be a very decadent and sometimes dangerous way to enjoy a relaxing drink. The combinations of flavours and textures seem never-ending and the classics are being constantly reinvented. I do love a good tomato juice, and the addition of vodka, with a hint of basil and celery, can only add to my happiness. I tend to drink them far too quickly, so making a sorbet slows down my consumption a little and means there is always a cocktail in the freezer when I feel the need to indulge. I serve them as a starter, a palate cleanser or even breakfast after a hangover.

Serves 4

200g granulated sugar
20 fresh basil leaves
100ml water
500g tomatoes, diced
1 celery stick, chopped
A squeeze of lemon juice
A splash of Worcestershire sauce
2 shots of vodka
Salt and freshly ground black pepper

○ Place half the sugar and the basil leaves into a processor and whizz quickly until the basil leaves are incorporated into the sugar, giving it a lovely green hue and wonderful smell.

Save it *Place 100g of the basil sugar into a lidded pot, jam jar or similar container and keep for tomorrow's cake.*

○ Tip the remaining sugar into a pan with the water and heat gently until the sugar dissolves, stirring occasionally, then boil for about 5 minutes to make a syrup. Leave to cool.

○ Using a hand blender, liquidiser or food processor, combine the tomatoes, celery, lemon juice, Worcestershire sauce and vodka. Blitz until you get a smooth purée. Rub the resulting purée through a sieve to remove any pips, skin or those nasty strings from the celery.

○ Stir in the cooled syrup. Taste and season with salt and pepper.

○ If you have an ice cream machine, spoon the mixture into the machine and churn until frozen. If not, pour the tomato mixture into a shallow tub, place in the freezer and stir every half hour or so until frozen.

Vary it *If you feel adventurous, make a Parmesan crisp cone or basket to serve this Bloody Mary sorbet in. Spoon some finely grated Parmesan into a pile on a baking tray and pop into a preheated oven at 190°C/gas 5, watching it carefully until just melted. Take it out of the oven and drape it over a cup to cool. Add a stick of celery to make it a veggie version of a 99 with a flake.*

Chocolate basil cake

There are some flavours that go together almost automatically: strawberries and cream, pork and apple, chips and ketchup. Others catch you out by how delicious they are: sea salted caramels or peanut butter and jam, but have you considered basil and chocolate? Trust me, it is just delicious. A wonderfully perfumed flavour that is just a little elusive on the palate. The deep, dark, rich chocolate provides a base layer for the fluting top notes of basil in this symphony of a cake.

Makes a 20 x 30cm cake

For the cake
150g plain flour
50g cocoa powder
100g golden syrup
100g basil sugar
100g butter
1 egg
125ml milk
1½ tsp bicarbonate of soda

For the chocolate basil ganache
300ml double cream
1 tbsp soft light brown sugar
10 fresh basil leaves
200g dark chocolate

Make the cake

○ Preheat the oven to 180°C/gas 4 and grease a 20 x 30cm cake tin.

○ Sift the flour and cocoa together into a large mixing bowl.

○ Pour the syrup into a saucepan and add the basil sugar and butter. Using a wooden spoon, stir the mixture over a gentle heat until the butter is melted. Remove from the heat and allow to cool slightly.

○ Break the egg into the milk and whisk together. Stir the bicarbonate of soda and the egg mixture into the cooled syrup and butter.

○ Stir all these ingredients into the sifted flour and cocoa, beating well to make sure the mixture is smooth. It will be lumpy to begin with but persevere.

○ Pour the mixture into the prepared tin and bake in the oven for 20–25 minutes until just firm. Turn out the cake on to a wire tray and leave to cool slightly.

Make and use the ganache

○ Place the cream, sugar and basil leaves into a pan and heat gently until the cream just bubbles at the very edge of the pan. Remove the basil leaves and pour the cream mixture over the chocolate. Stir and combine, trying your best not to lick the spoon during this procedure. Once the cream and chocolate have combined, allow to cool a little.

○ Cover the cake in a slick of delicious ganache and leave to set. You will have to wait to eat the cake so console yourself by licking out the bowl.

Shopping list

4 red chillies

6 corn cobs

1 onion

1 small bunch fresh chives

4-6 fresh sage leaves

8 chicken pieces

450g sausagemeat or sausages to be skinned

2 x 170g cans white crab meat

500ml buttermilk

4 tsp celery salt

1 cup breadcrumbs

500ml passata

From the storecupboard

Baking powder	Nutmeg
Black peppercorns	Oil - vegetable
Butter	Paprika
Eggs	Rice - basmati
Flour - plain	Stock
Garlic cloves	Sugar - caster
Milk	Wine vinegar - white
Mustard - wholegrain	

Crab cakes chain

It is said that the UK and the USA are two nations divided by a common language. Our food heritage has also followed a similar path, with its roots in the European tradition. However, influences from those we have had closest contact with have led our once very similar culinary DNA to evolve into two quite separate food species. This Crab cakes chain takes a trip across the pond.

Crab cakes with sweet chilli sauce → use a dollop or so of sweet chilli sauce to marinade the →
Southern fried chicken and corn cobs → strip the corn from the remaining cobs and make →
Sweetcorn buttermilk pancakes with sausage gravy → use up the additional sausages to make →
Baked sausage and tomato risotto

Crab cakes with sweet chilli sauce

I realise that most US crab cakes don't come with chilli sauce, but I like chilli sauce and so I'm adding it. If you'd rather have mayonnaise, then be my guest.

Serves 4

For the sweet chilli sauce
225g caster sugar
120ml water
120ml white wine vinegar
2 garlic cloves, chopped
4 red chillies, finely chopped

For the crab cakes
100g breadcrumbs
1 tbsp snipped fresh chives
½ tsp celery salt
½ tsp paprika
Freshly grated nutmeg
Freshly ground black pepper
2 x 170g cans white crab meat, drained
1 egg, beaten
½ tsp wholegrain mustard
Flour, for dusting
Oil, for frying

Make the chilli sauce

○ Place the sugar, water and vinegar in a large saucepan and heat slowly to dissolve the sugar.

○ Add the garlic and chillies and simmer to reduce the volume of the liquid by one-third. Leave to one side to cool.

Save it *Don't forget to save 2 tbsp sauce for the next recipe.*

Make the crab cakes

○ Combine the breadcrumbs, chives and spices in a bowl. Stir in the crab meat.

○ Whisk together the egg and the mustard. Add this to the crab and breadcrumb mixture one-third at a time until the mixture comes together but isn't wet and sloppy.

○ Divide into eight equal-sized balls, flatten slightly and coat with a little flour.

○ Heat the oil in a frying pan, and fry the crab cakes gently for about 5 minutes each side until golden and crisp.

○ Serve with a spoon of chilli sauce and 'have a nice day'!

Southern fried chicken with corn cobs

Fried chicken is such a guilty pleasure of mine. Not only do I often have to eat it with my fingers but you get to suck the meat off the bones in a way that just isn't acceptable at the Sunday dinner table. I am aware, however, that it isn't exactly the healthiest of dishes, even if you do go for a side of coleslaw! This recipe uses frying to crisp the outside of the chicken but the main cooking is done in the oven. Not perfect, I grant you, but good enough.

Serves 4

8 chicken pieces (thighs, drumsticks or breast portions)
Salt and freshly ground black pepper
500ml buttermilk
2 tbsp chilli sauce
1 garlic clove, crushed
Oil, for frying
8 tbsp plain flour
A pinch of smoked paprika
A little celery salt

To serve
6 corn cobs
Green beans
Coleslaw
Macaroni cheese (optional)

Cook the chicken

○ Take each chicken piece, wash and pat dry, then season with celery salt, salt and pepper. Place them in a non-metallic bowl. Add the chilli sauce to 350ml of the buttermilk, taste, and pour enough of the mixture over the chicken to cover it.

> **Save it** Put the rest of the buttermilk in the fridge for the pancakes.

○ Pop in the garlic at this point. Give the chicken a good massage. Cover with clingfilm and pop in the fridge for 2–10 hours or overnight.

○ Heat 1cm oil in a heavy-based frying pan. I use a cast iron skillet that I brought on the plane all the way from Texas – how I managed it, I shall never know!

○ Preheat the oven to 180°C/gas 4.

○ Put the flour in a plastic food bag, add the paprika and celery salt and season well with salt and pepper or your own special spice mix.

○ Shake some of the marinade off the chicken pieces, then place them into the flour-filled bag and toss to coat with flour.

○ Gently place the chicken pieces into the fat and cook for 3–4 minutes over a gentle heat until the outside begins to colour. Remove from the oil and place onto a rack on a baking tray. Bake for 20–30 minutes until the chicken is cooked through.

Finish and serve

○ Meanwhile, cook the corn cobs, green beans and make the coleslaw. If you want to go the whole hog, add a serving of macaroni cheese. See what I mean about divergent culinary DNA!

> **Save it** Put 2 corn cobs aside for tomorrow.

Sweetcorn buttermilk pancakes with sausage gravy

Fresh pancakes for breakfast are heavenly and not difficult at all, although don't let my children know that, as I tend to make a bit of a song and dance when they ask for them! Savoury pancakes such as these are ideal for a lazy Sunday brunch. Now that's another useful American invention for when the lie-in was longer than you intended.

Makes 12 pancakes

For the sausage gravy
100g sausagemeat
½ onion, finely chopped
25g butter
40g plain flour
400ml milk
Salt and freshly ground black pepper
Freshly grated nutmeg

For the pancakes
3 eggs
150ml buttermilk
180g plain flour
1½ tsp baking powder
Corn stripped from 2 corn cobs
Vegetable oil, for frying – use a flavourless oil

> **Save it** Use the sausagemeat from a 450g pack and save 300g for tomorrow, or you can skin a sausage from a pack of sausages if you prefer.

Make the gravy

○ Crumble the sausagemeat into a large saucepan and cook over a low heat for a few minutes until no longer pink. Stir in the onion and continue cooking until translucent.

○ Pop the butter into the pan and stir until melted, then sprinkle in the flour and stir well for several minutes over a low heat to lose the floury taste.

○ Gradually add the milk, whisking continuously until the only lumps in the sauce are because of the sausage. Season well with salt, pepper and a grating of nutmeg. Cover and keep warm whilst you cook the pancakes.

Make and serve the pancakes

○ Whisk together the eggs and the buttermilk in a deep bowl. Sift in the flour, baking powder and a pinch of salt and whisk to combine. Stir in the corn kernels.

○ Heat a large flat pan and smear with a small amount of a flavourless oil. Dollop a tablespoon of mixture onto the hot pan and cook on one side until the bubbles rise to the surface. Flip over and cook on the other side for a minute or so.

○ Place on a plate and smother in sausage gravy. Ugly but very, very tasty.

Baked sausage and tomato risotto

This is a hearty meal just right for a busy family evening. Baked tomato and sausage risotto will use up those unloved vegetables lurking in the vegetable rack, will stretch a few sausages into a family meal, and even use up that last slug of wine in the bottom of a bottle. Please feel free to adapt and change this recipe. If you'd rather use whole sausages and skin them, instead of buying sausagemeat, then that's fine too.

Serves 4

300g sausagemeat
Oil, for frying
½ onion, chopped
1 garlic clove, crushed
300g basmati rice
500ml passata
500ml stock
Salt and freshly ground black pepper
A few fresh sage leaves, finely shredded

To serve
Generous green salad

○ Preheat the oven to 180°C/gas 4.

○ Pinch off walnut-sized pieces of sausagemeat and roll them to form balls.

○ Heat a very small amount of oil in a frying pan and cook the sausage balls for a few minutes until the outside of the balls are coloured and a little crisp. Place the sausagemeat balls into a large gratin dish.

○ Now add the onion and garlic to the oil left in the frying pan and cook for a few minutes until translucent. If you have other vegetables to use up, now is the time to cook them a little.

○ Tip the vegetables into the gratin dish, then pour in the rice.

○ Add the passata and the stock and season well. I pour the stock into the passata carton to wash it out and to measure at the same time.

○ Scatter over the sage leaves. Give the whole thing a really good stir.

○ Cover with foil and bake in the oven for 35–45 minutes. Check after 20 minutes, stir and add more stock if you need to. If you have wine you could add a little of that. If you just have water, that's fine as well. The resulting dish should be sticky, tasty and just a little saucy.

○ Serve with a big green salad or with some steamed dark green leaves such as chard or cavalo nero.

Vary it You can add other vegetables such as mushrooms, courgettes, peppers or aubergine if you have them in your fridge. And it goes without saying that wine would also do in place of stock, but equally so would water. Use what you have; it will still fill everyone up.

Shopping list

1 lemon	600ml double cream
4 oranges	500ml vanilla custard
1 onion	4 anchovy fillets
600g floury potatoes	1 tsp capers
A handful of fresh basil	1 tsp chopped gherkins
1 bunch watercress	100g dark chocolate
4 steaks, the best you can afford	A few slugs of Cointreau
6 x 200g salmon pieces	

From the storecupboard

Baking powder	Mayonnaise
Breadcrumbs	Mustard - Dijon
Butter	Oil - olive and vegetable
Cocoa powder	Parsley - fresh
Eggs	Sugar - caster and icing
Flour - plain and selfraising	Vanilla powder or extract
Garlic	Wine vinegar - red

Poached salmon chain

Ideal for a more sophisticated picnic, possibly a warm summer evening barbecue or lazy Sunday lunch, this chain should suit both savoury and sweets lovers alike. Making your own mayonnaise is always worth it and as you have made the effort to create such a delicious dressing it makes sense to use up every scrap of it within these following recipes.

There is something of a summery vibe to the poached salmon chain.

Poached salmon with mayonnaise → Use up the salmon scraps, a little mayo and extra watercress to make →
Salmon and watercress fishcakes → the watercress left will add pepperiness to →
Steak with salsa verde → to follow your steak, use the leftover mayonnaise to make →
Chocolate mayonnaise cake → treat yourself to a nostalgia trip and enjoy **Proper trifle**

Poached salmon with homemade mayonnaise

Poaching salmon is quick and easy, and so is making your own mayonnaise. Don't be put off at all. If you really think it is too much trouble, then buy a good-quality mayonnaise and use that. I just ask that you to try making it once. That should be enough to have you hooked.

Serves 4

For the salmon
5 black peppercorns
Sea salt
½ lemon, thinly sliced
1 onion, thinly sliced
6 x 200g salmon pieces

For the mayonnaise
3 egg yolks
1 tsp Dijon mustard
About 400ml light olive oil

Save it *Freeze the egg whites and use them to make meringues, egg white omelette or marshmallows at a later date. They'll keep for three months in the freezer.*

To serve
Mixed green salad
¼ bunch watercress
New potatoes

Save it *Use the remaining watercress for the next two recipes.*

Cook the fish
○ Pour 2cm of water into a wide saucepan or frying pan and add the peppercorns, a good pinch of salt, the lemon and onion slices. Heat gently until warm but not boiling.

○ Lay the salmon pieces in the pan skin-side down. Keeping the poaching liquid just below simmering, cover the pan and leave for 15 minutes.

Save it *Keep 400g of the poached salmon for tomorrow.*

Make the mayonnaise

○ Whilst the salmon is poaching, place the egg yolks in a bowl and add the mustard and a pinch of salt.

○ To prevent the bowl flying across the room as you try to pour oil and whisk at the same time, I'd suggest enlisting child labour or, if they can't be bothered to put down the games controllers, then pop the bowl onto a damp tea towel. Slowly drizzle a thin stream of the oil into the egg yolks, whisking all the time. The mixture will gradually thicken and lighten in colour as the oil and egg yolk emulsify.

Save it Reserve 200g of the mayonnaise to make the cake and a little for the fishcakes.

○ Taste the remaining mayonnaise and season with salt and pepper.

Finish and serve

○ Lift the salmon carefully from the poaching liquid and serve with a large dollop of mayonnaise, boiled new potatoes and a green salad. A little watercress mixed in with the salad will add a delicious pepperiness.

Salmon and watercress fishcakes

You could, of course, just use up the left over poached salmon and watercress to make some really tasty sandwiches – I wouldn't dream of trying to stop you – but I have a problem in my house that sandwiches are seen as lunch food and dinner must be cooked. You might have had the mother of all lunches but you still need cooked food later, apparently. Salmon and watercress fishcakes are quick, easy and fit the remit of being cooked food very nicely.

Serves 4

600g floury potatoes, peeled and cut into chunks
Salt and freshly ground black pepper
1 large knob of butter
400g poached salmon
½ bunch watercress, finely chopped
2 tbsp mayonnaise
1 egg, beaten
4 tbsp plain flour
6 tbsp breadcrumbs
Oil, for frying

To serve
Chips
Salad
Mushy peas

○ Place the potatoes in a large pan of cold water and bring to the boil. Boil for about 15 minutes, depending on size, until soft, then remove from the heat, drain and allow to steam in the pan for a few moments to dry out the potatoes before mashing.

○ Mash the potatoes well, adding a good pinch of salt and the butter. Set to one side to cool a little.

○ Flake the cold poached salmon into a large bowl, stir through the chopped watercress and add the slightly cooled mashed potatoes. Add the mayonnaise ½ tbsp at a time, mixing until the mixture binds enough to shape into eight to 12 patties.

○ Put the beaten egg into a bowl, the flour in another and the breadcrumbs in a third. Coat the patties in a very light dusting of flour, dip into the egg and then finally coat in the breadcrumbs. Place on a baking tray and firm up in the fridge for half an hour.

○ Heat the oil in a wide frying pan, and fry the patties over a medium heat for 4–5 minutes each side until golden and crispy. Drain on kitchen paper.

○ Serve with chips, salad or mushy peas; I'll leave that up to you.

Steak with salsa verde

I do love a good steak, well-aged, with a decent marbling of fat. Buy the best steak you can afford. Look for the marbling through the steak as this gives it flavour and added succulence. Hopefully it will be just shown the barbecue until it's lovely, rare and juicy. Add to that a warm summer evening, a glass of red wine, a pile of matchstick chips and some salsa verde and I could well be in heaven. Join me!

Serves 4

For the steaks
Oil, for frying
1 garlic clove, crushed
4 steaks
Salt and fresh ground black pepper
A knob of butter
40g watercress

For the salsa verde
A handful of fresh parsley
A handful of fresh basil
1 tsp capers
1 tsp chopped gherkins
4 anchovy fillets
1 tsp mustard
2 tbsp red wine vinegar
8–10 tbsp cold pressed virgin olive oil

To serve
Chips or sauté leftover potatoes
Steamed baby corn

Cook the steaks

○ Leave a heavy-based frying pan to get to a good high heat but not quite smoking. I use a cast iron skillet but any heavy-duty pan will do. If you are tempted to risk the barbecue, get it white hot and take an umbrella.

○ Put a slug or two of oil into the pan, enough to coat the pan without any depth of oil remaining. Toss in the flattened garlic clove and fry to flavour the oil for a minute, but remove the garlic before it burns.

○ It is really important to season the steaks well with salt and pepper before you lay them in the pan. Do not move the steak around the pan but leave to cook for 1½–3 minutes on the first side. Turn and repeat this on the second side. At this point, add the butter. It won't help the cooking process but it makes the steak taste fantastic. These timings will give you a steak that is almost mooing at 1½ minutes to virtually cremated at 3 minutes per side.

○ Remove the steak to a warm plate and allow to rest; this is vital as it allows the meat to relax and, providing you bought well, it will become almost butter-like in texture.

○ While the steaks relax, make the salsa verde.

Make the salsa verde

○ Chop together all the dry ingredients. Stir in the mustard, red wine vinegar and plenty of the good olive oil. The consistency needs to be thinner than mayonnaise but thicker than a salad dressing.

Finish and serve

○ Serve the steaks with a good dollop of salsa verde, which will set them off a treat. It's brilliant to dip the chips or sauté potatoes in too. Steam some baby corn to serve alongside.

Chocolate mayonnaise cake

I know, but suspend your disbelief for a moment and think logically. Cakes almost always contain eggs and a fat. In a chocolate mayonnaise cake, the eggs and oil have simply been combined before being added to the other ingredients rather than during the mixing process. Trust me, the cake is chocolatey and moist. No one needs to know the secret ingredient – unless you wish to tell them, that is.

Makes an 18cm cake

300g self-raising flour
1½ tsp baking powder
225g caster sugar
200g mayonnaise
4 tbsp cocoa powder
250ml boiling water
1 tsp vanilla powder or extract

For the chocolate buttercream
150g butter, softened
25g cocoa powder
175g icing sugar, plus extra for dusting (optional)

Make the cake

○ Preheat the oven to 180°C/gas 4 and grease and line an 18cm, deep, loose-bottomed cake tin.

○ Sift the flour, baking powder and caster sugar into a large bowl. Take a deep breath and mix in the mayonnaise.

○ Dissolve the cocoa in the boiling water. Leave to cool a little, then add to the other ingredients in the bowl. Finally beat in the vanilla, then scrape into the prepared tin.

○ Bake in the centre of the oven for 1–1¼ hours until springy to the touch. Leave to cool in the tin, then turn out.

Make the icing and finish the cake

○ Beat together the chocolate buttercream ingredients. Spread over the top of the cake, and dust with a little sifted icing sugar if you like.

○ Put the kettle on and cut yourself a big slice. Don't think about the mystery ingredient.

Save it *Save half the cake to make a trifle.*

Proper trifle

There must be as many versions of trifle as there are mothers and grandmothers, and we all know they make the best and booziest trifles. It is time to put yourself amongst the greats and create a trifle of your own. As far as I'm concerned, a trifle cannot contain jelly, nor can it contain bananas, but if you really have to slice a few circles of that fruit, then you can. As the basis for my trifle is a chocolate cake, I'm sticking to oranges and orange liqueur. Cherries are great too, if you feel like creating a Black Forest version. If the season is right, use blood oranges — they will add a beauty to this dish that only nature can provide.

Serves 8

100g dark chocolate bar (I'll use a Green and Blacks Maya Gold for this orange trifle)
½ chocolate mayonnaise cake, sliced
A slug of Cointreau
500ml vanilla custard
4 oranges, peeled and segmented
600ml double cream, whipped

○ Melt ³/₄ of the bar of chocolate and put the rest in the freezer; it makes grating the bar less messy.

○ In Nan's best trifle bowl, make a layer of half the cake slices. Slosh over a good slug of Cointreau and cover with half the custard. Layer on half the orange segments, then create a layer with half the cream. Drizzle all the melted chocolate over the cream layer. Lick the spoon and the bowl containing the melted chocolate.

○ Repeat the layers again: cake slices, Cointreau, custard, oranges and cream. Grate the remaining chocolate over the top of the finished trifle.

○ Take a large spoon and serve. Do not drive anywhere too soon as this can be a very boozy dessert.

Cook's tip As I said in the introduction, variations of trifle are endless. You can substitute almost any flavour of cake into trifle if you have some left over. Ginger cake can be paired with cooked and cooled rhubarb; walnut cake is an ideal foil for apple purée; coffee cake and chocolate custard would make a great mocha version of this dish.

Shopping list

2 lemons
8 tomatoes
4 little gem lettuces
200g green beans
50g pea shoots
4 large mushrooms
2 large Maris Piper potatoes
1kg new potatoes
8 bacon rashers
½ black pudding link
4 sausages
4 slices of bread
300g sausagemeat
6 tuna steaks
12 eggs
6 anchovy fillets
125g black olives

From the storecupboard

Brown sauce
Eggs
Garlic clove
Oil – vegetable and olive

Panko breadcrumbs
Tomato ketchup
Wine vinegar – red

Tuna chain

British summertime is a fickle thing, here in March and then gone by April, occasionally sometimes finally putting in an appearance later in October. The grilled tuna chain is for just such confused times.

This chain is a real mixture of meals to warm you up, keep you going and possibly, if you are feeling brave, take on a picnic.

Grilled tuna steaks → use the additional tuna steak to flake into a →
Salade Niçoise → cooled boiled potatoes from yesterday's salad are sautéed to add to →
A full English breakfast → mix the half link of black pudding left into the remaining sausages and make a coating for →
Scotch eggs

Grilled tuna steaks

Simplicity is the name of the game here. If the sun is out, you can fire up the barbecue to start this chain; if not, a griddle pan or a dry frying pan will do just as well. The dry pan won't give you the nice char lines but that is all about looks, while taste is what is really important here. I'd suggest serving this with matchstick chips and a crispy pea shoot salad. Posh fish, chips and peas really!

Serves 4

For the chips
2 large or 4 small Maris Piper potatoes
Vegetable oil, for deep frying
Sea salt and freshly ground black pepper

For the tuna
6 tuna steaks, fresh or frozen, defrosted
1 lemon, quartered
Olive oil, for rubbing the tuna
For the dressing
Juice of ½ lemon
3 tbsp olive oil

To serve
1 bag of pea shoots or pick your own if you grow peas.

Cook the chips
○ Peel the potatoes and square off the edges. Cut the potatoes into slices about 3mm thick. Cut these slices again into matchstick lengths of the same thickness. Pop into a bowl of cold water for half an hour to get rid of the starch.

○ Drain the chips well and pat dry on kitchen paper.

○ Heat the oil in a large, deep pan; don't use a small pan as the chips will bubble up in the hot oil. Bring the oil to 180°C, when the surface will shimmer and the oil will almost smoke.

○ Rinse the matchsticks and pat dry on kitchen paper. Fry, a handful at a time, for about 2 minutes until golden brown. Drain on paper, sprinkle with sea salt flakes and keep warm. Smoked sea salt works wonderfully here if you have some.

Cook the tuna

○ Meanwhile, heat the barbecue, if you are using it, or the griddle if you are using it.

○ Allow the tuna to come to room temperature. Rub the tuna steaks on both sides with olive oil and season with some freshly ground black pepper. Lay the tuna gently into the pan or onto the barbecue, and cook as you would for any steak: rare, medium or well done. Watch it like a hawk. Tuna cooks when you turn your back on it. As soon as the edges are seared, remove and rest whilst you plate up. The steak will continue to cook as it rests, giving you time to serve the accompaniments.

Save it Put two steaks aside for tomorrow.

Finish and serve the dish

○ Whisk together the dressing ingredients and season with salt and pepper.

○ Plate up the tuna steak with a handful of the matchstick fries and the same of pea shoot salad, dressed with the olive oil and lemon juice dressing. This is one plate of fish, chips and peas that probably doesn't need ketchup but if you really must, then go on.

Save it Once cool, the remaining cooked tuna can be placed in an airtight container and kept in the fridge for the next day.

Salade Niçoise

In the same way that cream tea makers in the south west of England have signature jams and family scone recipes, which are pored over at WI events, all over the south of France, groups of men discuss exactly what constitutes a good salade Niçoise whilst playing *petanque*. The ladies, naturally, are the ones out buying the ingredients. The basic salad must include boiled potatoes, tuna, black olives, hard-boiled eggs, green beans and some tomatoes. The rest is up to its maker.

This is my recipe, not discussed with anyone playing boules. I'm far more likely to ask the ladies shopping in the market for tips anyway!

Serves 4

For the dressing
6 anchovy fillets
1 garlic clove, crushed
6 tbsp olive oil
1 tbsp lemon juice
1 tbsp red wine vinegar
Freshly ground black pepper

For the salad
1kg small new potatoes, boiled and cooled
200g green beans, boiled and cooled, you want them still to have a snap
4 little gem lettuce, quartered
4 tomatoes, quartered
4 eggs, boiled for about 6 minutes and then plunge into iced water and shelled
125g black olives – pitted are safest but just use your favourites
2 cooked tuna steaks
1 lemon, cut into wedges
Salt and freshly ground black pepper

Save it Place one-third of the potatoes in a container and put in the fridge to use within a couple of days, or freeze on an open tray, then put into a bag once quite solid to prevent them from sticking together, and freeze for up to two months.

Make the dressing

○ Pound together the anchovies, garlic and olive oil in a pestle and mortar and work to a smooth paste. Try not to add any salt as the anchovies should make the dressing salty enough.

○ Whisk in the lemon juice and red wine vinegar. Season to taste with pepper.

Make the salad

○ Halve the remaining cooled boiled potatoes and divide among four deep bowls. Divide the green beans among the bowls.

○ Pour a little of the dressing over the beans and potatoes and toss gently with your hands.

○ Tuck the gem lettuces, tomatoes and eggs into the beans and potatoes. Make it look attractive but not too constructed. Scatter over the olives. You can either slice or tear the tuna into the salad.

○ Allow the diner to season their own salad with lemon juice, salt, pepper and more dressing, if required.

Vary it *Salade Niçoise lends itself magnificently to frugality. You can use up sun-dried tomatoes instead of fresh; tinned tuna is perfectly acceptable; and the addition of some cooked haricot beans would be just fine to eke out the tuna, if needed.*

Full English breakfast

Yesterday you had a salad, so today balance must be restored. You need to top up those calories with a proper full English breakfast. Once again, this is one of those meals where it is possible to argue for days as to which elements are essential and which are mere frippery. You only have to pop your head around the door of a greasy spoon café and glance up at the menu board to see what I mean. Fried slice? Bubble? Tinned tomatoes or beans, but not both, and occasionally chips to round off the dish. All washed down with a mug of tea and garnished with a toasted doorstep. Ask nicely and they may cut the toast into triangles for you just to make it look dainty.

Serves 4

4 sausages
8 bacon rashers
½ link of black pudding, sliced into 1cm thick rings
4 large tomatoes, halved
4 large mushrooms
4 cups of tea
2 tbsp vegetable oil
400g cold cooked potatoes, halved
4 eggs
4 thick slices of bread
Salt and freshly ground black pepper
Ketchup and brown sauce to taste

Save it *Keep the other ½ link of black pudding in the fridge for tomorrow.*

o Heat the oven to 150°C/gas 2. Turn on the grill to medium.

o Put the sausages on the grill and grill for 10 minutes, turning regularly. Add the bacon and black pudding and continue to grill for 5 minutes, then add the tomatoes and mushrooms and grill until everything is cooked how you like it.

o As the items are cooked, transfer them to a baking dish, cover with foil and keep them warm in the oven.

o Make a pot of tea. Strong enough to support an upright spoon is usually the order of the day in a café but you are in charge here. I probably wouldn't recommend Earl Grey with these robust flavours, to be honest.

o Heat the oil in a frying pan until the oil begins to shimmer, Add the cold cooked potatoes and fry, turning with a fish slice to prevent them from burning but allowing them to make those lovely crusty edges that catch the runny yolk from an egg so perfectly. Once almost warmed through, make the eggs.

o Bring a pan of water to barely simmering point, break in the eggs and poach for 3 minutes. Lift out with a slotted spoon and drain on kitchen paper.

o Put the toast into the toaster and begin to assemble the dish.

o Put the bacon, sausage and black pudding onto the plate, the grilled tomatoes and potatoes to one side and the poached egg snuggled neatly on top of the toast.

o Pour yourself a cup of tea and decide red sauce, brown sauce or no sauce at all.

Scotch egg

One thing you can't trust in the UK is the weather. You could plan to cook the tuna on the barbecue, perhaps eat the salad outside and even indulge in a full English sitting on the patio, but your intentions may well be scuppered. A scotch egg is a wonderful dish as happy indoors as out, with champagne at a picnic or with a beer at the bar. All you have to decide is which venue you would prefer.

Makes 4

300g sausagemeat (getting your favourite sausages, skinning them and squeezing out the sausagemeat is the best way to do this, I find)
100g black pudding, finely chopped
Salt and freshly ground black pepper
4 eggs, boiled for 6 minutes, cooled in iced water and peeled

To coat and fry
3 tbsp plain flour
1 egg, beaten
1 bowl of panko breadcrumbs
Oil, for deep-frying

○ In a large bowl, mix together the sausagemeat and the black pudding. Season with salt and pepper and add any seasonings you want at this stage.

> **Vary it** If your sausages are plain and you want to add more flavour, now is the time to rasp in some nutmeg, add a little chopped sage or perhaps a dollop of mustard.

○ Take a quarter of the sausage mixture and lay it on a piece of clingfilm. Press out until about 1cm thick. Place an egg in the middle and gently mould the sausagemeat around the egg until the whole egg is encased. Repeat with the remaining eggs.

○ Put the flour, egg and breadcrumbs in separate bowls. Heat the oil in a deep-fat fryer or heavy-based saucepan to 160°C, when a cube of bread will brown in 80 seconds.

○ Roll the eggs in the flour, dusting off any excess, then in the egg and finally the breadcrumbs. Try to keep one hand for the wet ingredients and one for the dry otherwise your hands end up looking like they belong to the Incredible Hulk!

○ Gently slide the coated egg into the oil and cook for about 6–7 minutes. You may well need to turn the egg in the oil as it cooks to ensure an even colouring to the breadcrumb.

○ Remove from the pan, drain and allow to cool a little before slicing in half to admire your handiwork. Consume with enthusiasm and gusto.

Shopping list

1 lemon

1 carrot

1 celery stick

2 onions – preferably red

8 large floury potatoes for roasting

A few basil leaves

4 fresh rosemary sprigs

1 large chicken

6 slices salami

250g ball of Mozzarella

500ml passata

From the storecupboard

Breadcrumbs

Butter

Eggs

Flour – plain and strong white bread

Garlic cloves

Oil – olive and vegetable

Rice – Arborio

Sugar – caster

Wine – white

Yeast – dried

Roast chicken chain

There is a distinctly Italian feel to this chain and rightly so. Italian mothers and grandmothers from Naples to Chicago have long advocated that every ingredient must contribute something to a meal or it won't be purchased. Wasting food is frowned upon, so much so that as a nation they gave us ricotta, an inspiration to the frugal chef, a cheese made from the whey leftovers that in the UK we fed to pigs. This chain is as close as I'm going to get to being an Italian *Nonna* without jumping on a Vespa and ignoring traffic signals. Come along for the ride, bring the family!

Roast chicken → use the stock from the chicken carcass to make →
Chicken risotto → use the remaining cold risotto, add some mozzarella and a sauce to make →
Arancini → take the additional tomato sauce and the remaining mozzarella and make →
Pizza Margarita

Roast chicken

The best roast chicken I have ever eaten was bought from an open-fronted shop on the Italian island of Ischia. A wood-fired rotisserie cooked the chickens to perfection whilst the luscious juices dripped down onto the trays of potatoes below. Spears of rosemary filled the chicken cavities, perfuming the whole area with a heady aroma. I can't replicate the wood-fired rotisserie, if you have one I'm on my way round. But the flavours and potatoes we can but try.

Serves 4–6

1.5kg chicken
8 large floury roasting potatoes, peeled and cut into 6–8 pieces
Olive oil
Salt and freshly ground black pepper
1 lemon, quartered
4 garlic cloves, flattened with a knife or with the heel of your hand.
4 rosemary sprigs, about 10cm long – grow your own, it's cheaper!

To serve
Green salad
Tomatoes, thinly sliced

○ Preheat the oven to 190°C/gas 5. Allow the chicken to come to room temperature.

○ Blanch the potatoes in boiling salted water for 2–3 minutes. Drain and allow to steam for a moment or two.

- Take a large roasting tin with a rack and wipe the bottom of the tin with a little olive oil to prevent the potatoes from sticking to the bottom of the pan. Season the pan with salt and pepper.

- Place the parboiled potatoes in the base of the roasting tin and lay the rack on top, making sure the potatoes are not crushed.

- Put the chicken on top of the rack. Insert the lemon wedges, crushed garlic cloves and rosemary sprigs into the chicken cavities. Remember chickens have a neck cavity so fill that too! Massage 1 tbsp olive oil into the chicken, using your hands please, no time for squeamishness, (Remember *Nonna* will send the boys round if you mess up.) Season the chicken well with salt and pepper and place in the oven.

- Roast for 20 minutes per 500g plus 20 minutes until the juices run clear from the thickest part of the thigh when pierced with a knife.

- Once cooked, remove from the oven, cover in foil and leave to rest for 15 minutes. Increase the oven temperature to 220°C/gas 9 and blast the potatoes for 10–15 minutes until crispy.

- Serve the chicken and potatoes family style on a big platter so everyone can help themselves. Add a big green salad, some very ripe thinly sliced tomatoes and a large glass of something cold and Italian.

Save it *Reserve the carcass and all leftover meat for the next recipe.*

Chicken risotto

Cold roast chicken is a godsend; you can make a whole raft of things from a coronation chicken sandwich to chicken and ham pie. One thing that is often overlooked is that the carcass of the chicken makes the most fantastic stock. Endlessly useful, it can very economically fill an empty stomach and, with the addition of a few noodles, can almost certainly cure colds. If you don't have time to make stock straight away, freeze the carcass and make the stock later. Take any large pieces of chicken off the carcass before making the stock and use them in the risotto. Save any Parmesan rinds you may have and pop them in the freezer too. Add them to your chicken risotto as it cooks: it increases the depth of flavour substantially.

Serves 6

For the chicken stock
1 chicken carcass, with the garlic, lemon and parsley removed
1 onion, halved
1 carrot, halved
10 black peppercorns
1 celery stick, quartered
1 tsp salt

For the chicken risotto
1 tbsp olive oil
2 tbsp butter
1 red onion, finely chopped
450g arborio rice
300ml white wine
1.2l hot chicken stock
Cold chicken picked from the carcass before making the stock, cut into bite-sized pieces
A little Parmesan rind or fresh Parmesan

Make the stock

○ Place the chicken carcass in a large pan with the vegetables and seasoning. Fill the pan with water to cover the carcass and bring slowly to a simmer.

○ Skim off any fat or scum that rises to the surface. Continue to simmer, uncovered, for 3–4 hours.

○ Strain into a bowl and allow to cool. Cover.

Save it *This will keep for two days in the fridge or can be frozen for up to two months.*

Make the risotto

○ In a large saucepan, melt a spoonful of butter with the tablespoon of olive oil and fry the onion until soft. Cascade in the rice, turning it around in the buttery onion mixture until each grain is coated and becomes translucent. This will take about 2 minutes.

○ Pour in the wine and bring to a simmer, stirring constantly for about 3 minutes until the wine has reduced.

○ Start to add the hot chicken stock to the rice a ladleful at a time, stirring. Add the Parmesan rind now if you have one. Stir as you go and add more stock as the rice absorbs each new addition. After 20–25 minutes the rice should be creamy and thick but still have a bite to it. Stir in the chopped chicken and allow to heat through. Add the remaining butter to give the risotto a gloss.

○ Serve in a large bowl with a good shaving of parmesan and black pepper. The large pepper mill and suggestive grinding action is optional.

Save it *Reserve two portions of risotto to make the arancini.*

Arancini with tomato sauce

Either as a snack lunch with a bowl of salad, a bite to line the stomach before a beer or purchased from a deli just to keep you ticking over, arancini are addictive. Every Italian household has its own variation on both fillings and risotto flavours. Make this dish your own, then at least you can join in the animated discussions on whose is better, mine or yours.

Makes 8 arancini

For the arancini
2 portions of risotto (made from 150g rice), chilled
250g ball of mozzarella
4 slices of salami, quartered
50g plain flour
2 eggs, beaten
50g panko breadcrumbs
Salt and freshly ground black pepper
Oil for deep-frying

For the tomato sauce
1 tbsp olive oil
500ml passata
1 garlic clove, crushed
1 tsp sugar
Torn fresh basil

Make the arancini
○ Divide the cold risotto into 8 portions, and pinch 8 marble-sized lumps of cheese from the mozzarella ball. Have the salami to hand.

Save it *Wrap the rest of the mozzarella and salami in clingfilm and store in the fridge for another meal.*

○ Put the flour in one bowl, the egg in a second and the breadcrumbs into a third, seasoning with salt and pepper.

○ Take one portion of the risotto in your hand, form a ball and then poke the 2 quarters of the salami and a pinch of mozzarella into the rice ball. Form the rice around the filling until completely covered. Roll in the flour, then the egg and finally the breadcrumbs. Repeat the egg and breadcrumbs (not the flour) and pop onto a plate. Repeat this for the remaining portions.

○ Refrigerate for at least an hour.

Make the tomato sauce
○ Warm the olive oil and crushed garlic in a pan. Don't heat this too violently as the garlic will burn and taste bitter. Once the kitchen begins to smell of the Mediterranean, add the passata and combine well with the garlicky olive oil. Season with the salt, pepper and sugar. The sugar should heighten the tomato flavour, not sweeten the dish, so taste as you go.

○ Leave the sauce to simmer gently until reduced by half. Taste and season with salt and pepper.

Save it Divide the sauce in half and put one portion aside. Once cold, the sauce can be frozen for up to month for use later. Pop into a takeaway box or sealed plastic bag. Defrost at room temperature overnight.

○ Tear several basil leaves into the other serving, dip in your arancini, wave your arms around and discuss who should win Serie A this year!

Cook the arancini
○ Heat the oil to 160°C when a cube of bread will brown in 80 seconds. Deep-fry the arancini for 3–4 minutes until golden brown and crispy. Drain on kitchen paper and serve hot with tomato sauce.

Pizza Margarita

When it comes to pizza, I am a purist. Wood-fired, thin, crispy and fresh. Not for me the crispy duck and spring onion toppings or a three-cheese stuffed crust. I might run to a few slices of salami or prosciutto but that's it. I know the arguments (mostly from my children) that if putting chips and hotdogs on a pizza is good enough for the Neapolitans, then it's okay for us too. However, I won't be swayed. If you feel the need, please indulge yourselves, but if I catch you then you will be in trouble!

Serves 4

For the pizza dough
300ml warm water
1 tbsp sugar
10g dried yeast
A large pinch of salt
500g strong white bread flour, plus extra for dusting
25ml olive oil

For the topping
Tomato sauce
About 150g mozzarella
Salami
A few fresh basil leaves
Salt and freshly ground black pepper
Extra virgin olive oil, for drizzling

Make the dough

○ Pour half the warm water into a large jug. Add the sugar and the yeast and give a brisk stir. Leave in a warm, draught-free place to allow the yeast to activate and become frothy.

○ Sift the flour into a roomy bowl; add the salt and the oil. Once really frothy, pour in the yeast mixture and two-thirds of the remaining water. Using one hand, make a claw shape and gradually combine the flour and the liquids. Slowly add the remaining tepid water until the dough is formed. It should be soft to the touch, and neither dry nor sticky.

○ Flour your work surface and knead the dough for 5–10 minutes. The texture of the dough will change from being a little rough and dense to much smoother and softer as the gluten is worked.

○ Pop back into the bowl, cover with a clean tea towel and leave for an hour or so until doubled in size.

○ Return to your risen dough; give it a thump in the middle to knock it back. Divide the dough into four balls and leave to rise again for 30 minutes.

Create and cook the pizza

○ Heat the oven to 240°C/gas 9 and lightly oil two or three baking sheets.

○ Roll out the dough into four disks. Spread thinly with the tomato sauce from yesterday. Scatter over the mozzarella and the basil leaves. Okay, salami if you have to! Give a good grind of black pepper.

○ Slide into the oven and bake for 10 minutes or so. Drizzle with olive oil and eat with your hands.

Shopping list

½ cucumber

1 large butternut squash

1 onion

3 carrots

200g fine green beans

4 tomatoes

1 lemon

1 small bag mixed salad leaves

1 small bunch fresh coriander

1 small bunch fresh parsley

Fresh thyme

8-12 chicken thighs

2 tbsp tahini

2 x 410g cans chickpeas

1 small pack za'atar

From the storecupboard

Bicarbonate of soda	Oil – olive and vegetable
Chilli flakes	Paprika
Cinnamon	Sugar – caster
Cumin – ground	Wine – white
Flour – strong white bread	Yeast – fast-action dried
Garlic cloves	

Spiced chicken chain

Time is precious; it is up to you how you use it. I love having the opportunity to take a whole day to prepare and cook a meal for friends and family to share. Realistically this doesn't happen too often, given my role at home also encompasses cab driver, secretary, wardrobe mistress as well as room service. I do have to resort to food you can just bung in the oven.

A distinctly Middle Eastern flavour links the elements of this spiced chicken chain together. If you have never used za'atar or sumac before I'd urge you to try some. I can get it at my local large supermarket but local speciality shops are best as they will often give you recipe ideas too!

Spiced chicken and butternut squash bake → add the roasted squash to chickpeas, create your own flatbreads and make →
Butternut squash falafel wraps → using more chickpeas and the additional wraps whip up a bowl of →
Hummus and pitta chips

Spiced chicken and butternut squash bake

Serves 4

2 tbsp olive oil
1 large butternut squash, peeled and cut into chunks
1 onion, halved and thinly sliced
3 garlic cloves, flattened but not peeled
8–12 chicken thighs (this depends how hungry the hordes are)
1 tsp chopped fresh thyme
1 tsp cumin
½ tsp paprika
½ tsp chilli flakes
A pinch of ground cinnamon
Salt and freshly ground black pepper
1 glass of white wine, stock or water
200g fine green beans, topped and tailed and cut in half

To serve
Crusty bread

○ Preheat the oven to 200°C/gas 6. Oil the bottom of a large, heavy-based roasting tin with a tablespoon or so of olive oil.

○ Tip in the peeled and chopped pieces of squash, the onions and the flattened garlic cloves.

○ Place the chicken thighs in a bowl or a big plastic bag and add the herbs and spices, seasoning with salt and pepper. Combine well and then place on top of the vegetables.

○ Pop into the oven and bake for 35 minutes. After this time is up, remove from the oven, pour in the wine and stir through the green beans. Return to the oven and bake for a further 10 minutes. The wine will both steam the beans and make a sauce for the meal.

Save it *Reserve about 150g of the cooked and roasted butternut squash and the roasted garlic for the falafel.*

○ Serve the chicken and remaining vegetables in big bowls with hunks of crusty bread to soak up the juices.

Butternut falafel wraps

I know food on the go is castigated as one of the many reasons why society is imploding and children don't give up their seats on buses to the elderly any more, but falafel has been around since the Coptic Egyptians first celebrated Lent in around 100AD so perhaps we can allow it into our lives without fear of calamity. Handy for a weekend snack lunch, it is both filling and good for you.

Serves 4

For the flatbreads
450g strong white bread flour, plus extra for dusting
1½ teaspoons salt
1 tbsp sugar
7g fast-action dried yeast
2 tbsp olive oil
About 300ml warm water

For the falafel
410g can chickpeas, drained and washed
150g leftover roasted butternut squash
3 garlic cloves, roasted
1 small bunch fresh coriander chopped
1 small bunch fresh parsley, chopped
½ tsp bicarbonate of soda
Vegetable oil, for frying

To serve
Fresh cucumber
Tomatoes
Onion, thinly sliced
Lemon wedges

Make the flatbreads

○ Make the flatbreads first as they need time to rise and prove. Tip the flour into a large, roomy bowl, Stir in the salt, sugar and dried yeast. Put some extra water ready just in case you need it – otherwise you may need to find someone to blame for the mess. Me, perhaps? Combine the oil and measured water and pour into the flour. Mix well, using your hands, until everything binds together, adding a little more water if necessary.

○ Knead the dough for a good 10 minutes, or 5 in a food processor, until smooth and elastic; kneading dough is better than therapy and cheaper than the gym. Leave the dough in an oiled bowl to rise for about an hour or until doubled in size.

Make and cook the falafel

○ Place all the falafel ingredients in a bowl and, using a hand blender, whizz the ingredients together. The falafel mixture needs to be fairly smooth as you want it to form balls that won't break up when you fry them.

○ Use a spoon or an ice cream scoop to make sure your falafel are all the same size. That solves all those 'his is bigger than mine' arguments when it comes to portion size, I can tell you! Wetting your hand slightly and just squeezing the falafel gently will make sure they stay together when frying.

○ Heat a little oil in a frying pan and shallow-fry your falafel for a few minutes on each side until crisp and golden. Drain on kitchen roll and keep them warm.

Cook the flatbreads

○ Place a dry frying pan on the heat. Once the dough for the flatbreads has risen, pinch off 12 tennis ball-sized pieces, roll out to about 3mm thick and place onto the hot pan. The bread will puff and bubble, then turn over and cook on the other side for a moment more.

○ Take a warm fresh flatbread. Place a couple of falafel, some cucumber, tomato and onion salad and a squeeze of lemon juice. Eat and enjoy!

Save it *Make any remaining dough into flatbreads and save for the hummus dish that follows. You can freeze the baked flatbreads in a Ziploc bag interleaved with baking parchment.*

Hummus and pitta chips

After a busy day, the thought of a cold libation often keeps me going until I eventually manage to get home and put the key in the door. Cold drinks also call for a side dish to munch on. Hummus and pitta chips are both tasty and reasonably good for you too. It is those several glasses of wine tonight that might make tomorrow even more difficult than today!

Serves 4

For the pitta chips
4–6 pitta breads
Olive oil
Za'atar or sumac

For the hummus
400g can chickpeas, drained
3 tbsp olive oil
2 tbsp tahini
1 garlic clove, crushed
Juice of 1 lemon
Salt and freshly ground black pepper
1 tsp cumin
Za'atar or sumac, to sprinkle on the finished dish

Cook the pitta chips
○ Preheat the oven to 200°C/gas 6.

○ Take the pitta breads and cut them into quarters. Using a pastry brush, lightly oil the breads on one side. Place onto a baking tray and bake for 5–10 minutes. Watch this like a hawk; it has the same capacity for mischief as a stray labrador in the china department.

Make the hummus
○ Meanwhile, tip the chickpeas, olive oil, tahini, garlic and half the lemon juice into a bowl and blitz with a hand blender. Add more lemon juice to slacken the mixture if it needs it. Taste and season with cumin, salt and pepper.

○ Scrape the hummus into a bowl, drizzle with a little more olive oil, if you have it, and sprinkle with either sumac or za'atar. If you have neither of these, a pinch of smoked paprika on the hummus will do nicely.

Finish the dish
○ Remove the pitta chips from the oven and sprinkle with za'atar or sumac.

○ Pour that cold drink you were dreaming about, dip and dunk.

Shopping list

1 lemon

1 green chilli

10 jalapeño peppers

3 carrots

1 onion

A bunch of fresh tarragon

900g-1kg turkey breast steaks

300g cooked ham pieces

200g sweetcorn kernels

300ml chicken stock

50g Cheddar cheese

500g ready-made puff pastry

4 flour tortillas

Soured cream

Guacamole

Tomato salsa

From the storecupboard

Breadcrumbs

Butter

Eggs

Flour - plain

Stock

Garlic cloves

Milk

Oil - vegetable

Parsley - fresh

Turkey Kiev chain

Turkeys shouldn't just mark Christmas or Thanksgiving on their calendars: with this chain they should be worried all year round. If at Christmas you do have a plate of turkey left over, then start the chain at the turkey and ham pie stage. Keep your workload to a minimum over the holidays by using ready-made pastry.

Turkey Kiev → take the cooked turkey trimmings and with the addition of ham make →
Turkey and ham pie → use up the sweetcorn left from the pie to make →
Chilli and sweetcorn quesadillas → finish off the pack of peppers by transforming them into →
Jalapeño pepper poppers

Turkey Kiev

I am a sucker for food that has more than one texture. Kievs are a fantastic way to get at least three different texture sensations in one dish. The crisp exterior gives way to a soft tender layer of juicy turkey and then the buttery golden liquid in the middle usually explodes all over the plate. Add to that some crisp broccoli and smooth, smooth mash and you have a winner.

Serves 4

2 garlic cloves, chopped
1 tbsp chopped fresh parsley
200g butter, softened
Salt and freshly ground black pepper
4 x 200g turkey breast steaks
2 tbsp plain flour
1 egg, beaten
100g breadcrumbs
Oil, for frying

To serve
Mashed potatoes
Broccoli

Make the turkey Kievs
○ Heat the oven to 180°C/gas 4 and lightly grease a baking tray.

○ Crush the garlic to a purée with a little salt using the side of a large knife. Beat the garlic and parsley into the butter with a little black pepper. Roll the butter into a sausage shape in some clingfilm and freeze for 10 minutes.

○ Lay the turkey steaks on a piece of clingfilm, place another piece on top and GENTLY batten out a little. Put any turkey trimmings and any remaining pieces of turkey to one side for later.

○ Take the frozen butter from the freezer and divide into quarters. Place a piece in the middle of each steak and fold the turkey over to cover. Secure with cocktail sticks, if necessary.

○ Place the flour, beaten egg and breadcrumbs into separate bowls. Flour the turkey parcel, then dip into the egg and finally coat in breadcrumbs.

○ Heat about 2cm oil in a frying pan and gently fry the Kiev for 2–3 minutes on each side to allow them to become crisp and golden. Place on the prepared baking tray and bake for 20–25 minutes until cooked through.

Cook the trimmings
○ As the turkey bakes in the oven, drain the oil from the frying pan and cook the turkey trimmings, browning them in the pan. When cooked through, place to one side, cool and keep for the pie. As long as the turkey has not already been frozen, you can freeze the turkey trimmings uncooked to cook at a later date too.

○ Mash and broccoli go very well with these golden beauties.

Turkey and ham pie

I do love a pie! I am pretty certain I can trace this back to my love of school dinners. The way the steam curls up as you cut the crust from a pie is as good as a kiss on the cheek, in my opinion. The ham in the pie can come from leftover Christmas ham, some baked gammon or some of those ham ends they offer on many supermarket deli counters. The quantities are approximate.

Serves 4

50g butter
1 onion, finely chopped
3 carrots, chopped
100g canned sweetcorn, drained
25g plain flour
300g cooked turkey, cut into cubes
300g cooked ham, cut into cubes
550ml chicken stock
Salt and freshly ground black pepper
A handful of chopped fresh tarragon or parsley
A squeeze of lemon juice
450g ready-made puff pastry
A little flour, for dusting
1 egg, beaten, or a little milk, to glaze

Save it *Take from a can of sweetcorn and use the rest tomorrow.*

Make the filling
○ Preheat the oven to 200°C/gas 6.

○ Melt half the butter in a large pan and add the onion. Cook over a low heat for 10 minutes until soft but not coloured. Add the carrots and sweetcorn and toss in the butter onion mixture. Pour in 250ml stock and simmer gently until the stock has reduced almost to nothing. Spoon into the bottom of a pie dish.

○ Melt the remaining butter in a saucepan and stir in the flour. Keep stirring until the floury flavour has been cooked out. This will take no longer than 5 minutes. Gradually pour in the stock, whisking or stirring constantly to prevent lumps. When all the stock is combined, simmer gently for another 5 minutes.

○ Season your sauce with a good pinch of salt and freshly ground black pepper. Taste and check. A squeeze of lemon juice and a handful of chopped tarragon wouldn't go amiss either. Place the turkey and ham mixture into the pie dish and pour over the sauce. Give it a stir to combine the flavours.

Make and bake the pie
○ Roll out the pastry on a lightly floured surface. Top the pie with the pastry. Brush with egg or milk. Bake for 25–30 minutes or until the pie crust is risen and golden brown.

Chilli and sweetcorn quesadillas

Cheese on toast is a lifesaver. As a quick lunch, an after-school snack or a light supper, it is ready quickly and can be rustled up from the contents of most fridges. Oozing melted cheese pleases most people and a quesadilla is simply Mexico's take on finding a way to eat molten cheese without burning your fingers in the process.

Serves 1–2

100g sweetcorn
1 green chilli, finely chopped
4 flour tortillas
120g sharp Cheddar cheese, grated

To serve (optional)
Soured cream
Guacamole
Tomato salsa

○ I find it best to build a quesadilla in the pan you are using to cook it, as they are treacherous and can spill their contents everywhere if you try to carry them around uncooked.

○ Heat a frying pan, then lay a flour tortilla in the pan. Cover with half the grated cheese, sprinkle on half the sweetcorn and scatter with half the chopped chilli. Top with a second tortilla and allow to cook for 1–2 minutes until the cheese begins to melt.

○ Using a fish slice or spatula, turn the quesadilla over to cook on the other side for a further minute or so, then slide on to a plate and keep it warm while you make the second quesadilla.

○ Cut them into quarters and eat.

Accompany it *If the sun is over the yard arm, a Mexican beer or a margarita is the ideal accompaniment. If the day is still young a cup of chocolate is great too.*

Cook's tip *If wraps are not available to you but you have a bag of tortilla chips in the house, build a bowl of nachos. Into a large microwavable bowl layer the chips, cheese and sweetcorn. Scatter half the chopped chilli over the nachos and cook in the microwave in bursts of 30 seconds on high until the cheese is melted. Remove from the microwave and sprinkle over the remaining chopped green chilli.*

Jalapeño pepper poppers

Spicy snacks, mmmm. The wonderful thing about jalapeño peppers is that they seem genetically programmed to play culinary Russian roulette. Out of the blue, a really hot pepper sneaks itself into a packet of its milder cousins and threatens to blow your head off. It is, of course, funniest when this happens to someone else and not you!

Serves 4 – About 10 jalapeños

50g Cheddar cheese, very finely grated
1 tbsp finely chopped onion
100g plain flour, plus extra for dusting
1 egg
300ml milk
Oil, for shallow-frying

○ Using a griddle pan, a barbecue or a grill, char the peppers until the skin blisters and blackens. Pop into a bowl and cover with clingfilm to allow the peppers to steam. Leave for 20 minutes or so. As the peppers cool, the steaming allows the skin to be removed easily. Peel the peppers, make a slit in the side of the pepper and remove the seeds.

○ Combine the cheese and onion. Slide a spoonful of the mixture into each pepper, close with a cocktail stick and repeat for the other peppers.

○ Whisk the flour, egg and milk to make a batter.

○ Heat a little oil for shallow-frying in a frying pan. Dust each pepper in flour and pat off any excess. Dip the pepper into the batter and lower into the oil. Fry for a few minutes until golden brown on all sides. Drain on kitchen paper.

○ Serve quickly as these are best warm. What a pity if no one is around – you may have to eat them all by yourself!

Cook's tip *If you are feeling brave, don't remove the seeds before you add the cheese. Nachos and salsa, fresh guacamole and, surprisingly, big bowls of pork scratchings are all TexMex snacks that could accompany these poppers.*

Shopping list

1 red chilli – optional
1 bunch spring onions
1 tbsp chopped fresh coriander
1 carrot
25cm piece of fresh ginger
4 fresh figs
1 punnet blueberries
1 punnet raspberries
1 punnet strawberries
1 duck
400g rice noodles
300ml double cream
600ml natural yoghurt
Rice wine vinegar

From the storecupboard

Chinese five-spice powder
Eggs
Flour – plain
Honey
Milk

Oil – sesame and vegetable
Porridge oats
Soy sauce
Sugar – caster
Tomato ketchup

Duck chain

If fat is flavour, then duck fat surely must be amongst the richest, most decadent flavours of them all. I grant you that fat isn't fashionable but I'm not asking you to eat only duck fat, smear yourself with it or sell it on the black market. I'm suggesting you use it as a form of natural flavour enhancer – monosodium glutamate in gamey form if you will.

This is clearly a chain of two halves, the first half champions duck enriched with spicy Chinese seasonings. The second brings fruit and a lighter feel.

Warm roast duck and noodle salad → take some shredded duck, noodle and vegetables and roll yourself some →
Spring rolls → use up the egg whites not needed to make the spring roll wrappers to create →
Eton mess with mixed berries → add a tub of yogurt, some honey and a dash of ginger to the extra berries and hey presto you have →
Breakfast smoothies

Warm roast duck and noodle salad

To be honest, if you can't be bothered making a salad, just pop some par-boiled potatoes around the duck for the last 50 minutes of its roasting time. When you rest the duck, steam a few green vegetables and serve with the crispy duck meat for the most delicious roast potatoes in the world. A scattering of good sea salt should be all the adornment this meal needs.

Serves 4

For the duck
1 duck
Sea salt
Chinese five-spice powder

For the noodles
400g rice noodles
A few drops of sesame oil
1 bunch spring onions
4 fresh figs, quartered
A handful of chopped fresh coriander
For the dressing
2 tbsp ketjap manis

> **Save it** *Use 4 or 5 spring onions for this dish and save the remainder for the spring rolls.*

> Ketjap manis is a thick and slightly sweetened soy sauce that you can buy in oriental stores.

1 tbsp soy sauce
1 tbsp rice wine vinegar
1 red chilli, finely chopped (optional)

Roast the duck

○ Preheat the oven to 220°C/gas 7.

○ Place the duck onto a roasting rack over a deep roasting tray. Using a skewer, pierce the skin all over the duck. Pay particular attention to the areas that have the most fat just below the skin. This will allow the duck to baste itself, with the added advantage that the skin becomes beautifully golden and crispy in the process. Rub the skin with a good pinch of salt, just as if you were giving the duck an exfoliating treatment! Sprinkle all over with the five-spice powder.

○ Roast for 20 minutes per 500g plus an extra 20 minutes. Rest the duck for 20 minutes under a tent of foil.

○ Pour all the duck fat into a ramekin and keep to one side. Carve the duck and serve. Make sure all those who want a crispy shard of skin can have it.

Save it *Imagine the meat is to serve five and keep one fifth of the meat and skin to one side for the next dish, the spring rolls.*

Make the salad

○ Prepare the noodles as directed on the packet. Plunge into cold water to halt the cooking process. Drain and sprinkle with a few drops of sesame oil. Turn over with a fork to coat the noodles and stop them clumping into an amorphous mass.

Save it *Put one-quarter of the noodles in the fridge for the spring rolls.*

○ Slice the 4–5 spring onions lengthways, then mix with the remaining noodles. Arrange artfully on a large plate. Scatter over the slices of duck. Tuck the fig quarters into the noodles and around the duck. Play hide and seek with them, tease the diners!

Save it *Any extra duck can be used up tomorrow.*

○ Whisk together ketjap manis, soy sauce and rice wine vinegar and stir in the chopped chilli, if using. Drizzle over the salad. Scatter with coriander and serve.

Spring rolls

This is ideal as a light lunch dish, a starter or just to placate a group of hungry teenagers as they hunt and forage in the fridge for a between-snack nibble! If you have leftover salad dressing, this would make an ideal dip for the spring rolls too.

Makes 12 spring rolls

For the spring roll wrappers
2 egg yolks
60ml cold water
150g plain flour, plus extra for dusting

Save it *Keep the whites for the Eton mess tomorrow.*

Cheat it *If you can't be doing with this, most supermarkets sell spring roll wrappers.*

For the duck filling
Shredded duck meat
100g cold noodles
2 spring onions, sliced lengthways
1 carrot, finely grated
Salt and freshly ground black, pepper
A pinch of Chinese five-spice powder
Vegetable oil, for frying

To serve
Soy sauce
Sweet chilli sauce (see page 48)
Tomato ketchup
Mixed green salad

Make the pastry

○ Mix the egg yolks and water together, stir into the flour and combine. Using your hands to bring the dough together, knead until smooth, then leave to rest for at least 30 minutes in the fridge.

○ Shape the dough into a sausage, then divide into 12 equal portions. Take each piece and, using a rolling pin, roll out into circles on a lightly floured surface, with a diameter of about 15cm.

Make the filling

○ In a roomy bowl, toss together the filling ingredients. Season with a little salt, pepper and five-spice powder.

Vary it *If you have bean sprouts, water chestnuts, Chinese cabbage this could also be added to the mix at this point.*

Make and cook the spring rolls

○ Fill a small bowl with water.

○ Divide the filling equally among the wrappers, placing it lengthways across the wrapper and leaving a gap at the edges. Fold in the edges at the short sides of the filling. Roll up the wrapper from the bottom to make a cylinder containing the filling. Dampen your finger and use this to seal the top edge of the wrapper.

○ Repeat with the remaining wraps.

○ Heat the oil in a shallow frying pan until medium-hot. Carefully place the rolls in the pan and cook until golden brown and the filling is heated through, turning to cook evenly. Remember to cook only a few spring rolls at a time as overcrowding the pan causes the temperature of the oil to fall. No one likes a soggy spring roll.

○ Serve with a dip of soy sauce, sweet chilli sauce or ketchup if you are a philistine! A side salad would be nice too, unless you are the above-mentioned teens who will view this as an attempt at poisoning.

Eton mess with mixed berries

Eton mess is very simply a deconstructed pavlova. My theory is someone somewhere dropped a pavlova on the way to the table, scraped it up and served it as an Eton mess. I am not including an instruction to drop the dish from a great height but if you must, you must!

Serves 4

For the meringues
2 egg whites
120g caster sugar

For the Eton mess
1 tray of cold meringue
600ml double cream
1 punnet of strawberries, halved or quartered, if large
1 punnet of blueberries
1 punnet of raspberries

Save it *Reserve one-third of the strawberries, blueberries and raspberries for your breakfast smoothie.*

Make the meringue
○ Heat the oven to 150°C/gas 2. Cover a large baking tray with baking parchment and put to one side.

○ Whisk the egg whites until they form stiff peaks. Using a tablespoon, add the caster sugar 1 tbsp at a time, whisking as you go. The meringue will thicken and become glossier as you proceed.

○ Once all the sugar has been added, spread the meringue out over the baking tray in one uniform layer. It needs to be about 2cm deep all over.

○ Place in the oven, turn the oven down to 140°C/gas 1 and bake for an hour exactly.

○ After an hour, turn the oven off and leave the meringue to cool completely. Overnight is fine.

Assemble the mess

○ Break up the meringue but try to keep the pieces bigger than 15mm in diameter.

○ Whip the cream until it forms soft peaks, then fold together with the meringue. Gently fold in two-thirds of the strawberries, blueberries and raspberries.

Save it Pop the remaining berries in the fridge, use them for a smoothie, or pop them in a freezer container and freeze them for up to three months.

○ Serve quickly and eat greedily.

Vary it Do vary the berry mix if you want to, but just keep the quantities the same. But if the berries are BOGOF in the supermarket or you pick your own, then go with whatever you have.

Breakfast smoothies

This recipe is one of those ways where you can pretend that you are being a kind and loving parent but what you are really doing is waking the house up. After all, they have all been lying in too long, there's lots to do and you are hungry.

Serves 4

500g mixed berries
600ml natural yogurt
1 tbsp honey, or to taste (optional)
1 tsp grated fresh root ginger
3 tbsp porridge oats
A splash of milk

○ Rinse the berries, taste one and pop the rest into a blender. If you have a hand blender, then tip the berries into a large Pyrex jug.

○ Add the yogurt. If the blueberries were a little tart now is the time to add honey to taste. Add the porridge oats and stir well.

○ Grate the ginger onto a plate. Pick up the ginger and place it in the palm of your hand. Squeeze the juice out of the ginger pulp into your yogurty mixture. Discard the dry ginger pulp.

○ Using the blender or hand blender, pulverise the mixture until smooth. Thin the smoothie with milk until it reaches the consistency you prefer.

○ Reawaken the sleepers with a smile, the papers and list of chores for later.

Cook's tip You can be as creative as you want when making breakfast smoothies. Whatever you have in your fruit bowl can make an appearance, although citrus fruits need to be added judiciously. Strawberries and bananas are a classic mix; blackberry and apple is a lovely autumnal offering; grapes and kiwis will give your smoothie a slightly green hue. Don't forget your vegetables as well. Carrot, orange and ginger is another combination to perk you up in the morning.

Shopping list

1 lemon	500g sausages
1 lime	500g lamb mince
2 large tomatoes	1 tbsp grated coconut
1-2 green chillies	250-300g bag of sev-based snack
25cm piece fresh ginger	Bombay mix or similar
3 tbsp chopped fresh coriander	35g mini poppadoms
1 tbsp chopped fresh mint	Pomegranate molasses
5 large red onions	1 measure gin per drink
1 pomegranate	1l bottle of tonic

From the storecupboard

Butter	Lard or white vegetable fat
Chilli flakes	Milk
Cinnamon – ground	Nutmeg
Cumin – ground	Oil – olive and vegetable
Egg	Sugar – caster
Flour – plain and strong white bread	Wine vinegar – white
Garlic cloves	Yeast – dried

Hot dog chain

Life can be frenetic at times, rushing hither and thither. Gathering people or possessions from one place and depositing them elsewhere is very time consuming. I find that getting a meal organised that pleases everyone and doesn't resort to opening the microwave door is sometimes tricky. I have compiled a chain here that is filling and quick. I grant you that making hot dog buns takes time but plan ahead and pop them in the freezer or simply buy some from the bakers. No one will ever know! This is a great selection of dishes for a bonfire feast too.

Hot dogs in a bun with onions → keep some sweet sticky onions to make →
Lamb kofta kebabs with fresh chutney → use any remaining chutney to spice up →
Bhel puri → freeze the excess pomegranate seeds in cubes to add sparkle to →
Gin and tonic with pomegranate ice

Hot dogs in a bun with onions

I know, it all sounds like junk food but if you buy the best sausages you can, frankfurters or British bangers it doesn't matter, have good bread and go easy on the ketchup, then occasionally junk can be fun.

Serves 4

For the buns
330ml warm milk
1 tsp sugar
1 sachet dried yeast
650g strong white bread flour, plus extra for dusting
30g caster sugar
75g white vegetable fat or lard, diced
1 egg
1 tsp salt
Flavourless oil, for greasing trays

For the onions
A knob of butter
1 tbsp olive oil
4 large red onions, thinly sliced
2 tsp sugar
3 tsp white wine vinegar

For the sausages
450g sausages of your choice, Cumberland, Frankfurters, whatever!

Make the dough
○ Place 150ml of the warm water in a jug and stir in a sprinkle of sugar and the yeast. Leave out of any draughts until the yeast has doubled in size.

○ Into a large bowl, sift the flour and stir in the sugar and salt. Rub the vegetable shortening into the flour until it resembles breadcrumbs. Pour in the remaining warm milk and stir to begin to incorporate. Add the beaten egg and the yeast mixture. Using a round-bladed knife, mix until the dough comes together.

○ Using your hands, knead the dough gently but effectively for 5 minutes or so until the dough becomes smooth and silky. If the dough is very soft and 'loose', you may need more flour on your work surface as you work it.

○ Make the dough into a ball and place in an oiled bowl. Cover with a damp cloth. Leave for 1½ hours until well risen.

○ Knock back (punch the dough in the middle to deflate it) and let it rise again for another 45 minutes.

Cook the onions

○ The onions will take at least 30 minutes of slow and low cooking to get to the melting sweetness that makes them a vital component of this steak dish. In a large saucepan, melt the knob of butter with the oil over a high heat. Tip in the thinly sliced onions. Cook over a high heat until the onions just begin to caramelise, then turn the hob as low as it will go and leave to cook gently for 15 minutes.

○ Much of the liquid from the onions should have evaporated by now so add the sugar and vinegar. Cook for a further 15 minutes until golden brown and sticky.

○ Keep half the onions for the hot dogs.

Save it *Cool the remaining onions and keep in the fridge for the kofta recipe.*

Finish the dish

○ Meanwhile, preheat the oven to 190°C/gas 5.

○ Cook the sausages in the oven, if appropriate, or on the hob, depending on type.

○ On a lightly floured surface, divide the dough mixture into cricket ball-sized pieces. Roll out into sausage shapes and place on an oiled baking tray to rise again for another 15 minutes.

○ Bake in the oven for 15 minutes, then leave to cool. Either use immediately or once cool, put into a bag and freeze until needed.

○ Slice the buns, slide in a sausage, top with a spoon of meltingly soft onions and add condiments of your choice.

Lamb kofta kebabs with fresh chutney

These little lamb koftas can be made in a morning, refrigerated and then baked in the oven when needed later in the day. Baking the koftas not only makes them less greasy but also frees up your hands to chop and assemble the fresh chutney.

Makes about 24 koftas

For the kebabs
500g lamb mince
2 garlic cloves, puréed
2cm fresh root ginger, grated
Softened onions
1 tsp freshly ground black pepper
1 tsp ground cumin
½ tsp ground cinnamon
2–3 rasps of nutmeg
1 tsp chilli flakes
1 heaped tbsp plain flour or gram flour, to bind
Oil, for greasing

For the fresh chutney
1 red onion, diced
2 large tomatoes, deseeded and chopped
3 tbsp chopped fresh coriander leaves
1 tbsp chopped fresh mint leaves
1 green chilli, finely chopped (2 if you really like heat)
1 tbsp grated coconut
Juice of ½ lemon
Juice of ½ lime
Sea salt

To serve
Boiled rice

Save it Keep other half of the lime for the bhel puri.

Make the lamb koftas

○ Preheat the oven to 180°C/gas 4 and lightly oil a baking tray.

○ Put all the ingredients into a large bowl and use your hands to combine well. Form the mix into sausages, sausage shaped and sized.

○ Lay the koftas in the prepared baking tray and bake for 30–40 minutes.

Make the chutney

○ Leaving out the lemon and lime juices, chop and combine the remaining ingredients in a non-metallic bowl.

> **Save it** *Place half of this undressed chutney into the fridge for the bhel puri.*

○ When ready to serve, add the citrus juices and season to taste.

○ Serve the koftas with a healthy portion of plain boiled rice and a big spoon of the fresh chutney. Oh, and a beer!

Bhel puri

I am making no claims that this is an authentic recipe for bhel puri. It is my version, an amalgamation of the delicious snacks and titbits I have been fortunate enough to eat. Offered to me on my travels abroad and visits to the houses of friends, it is delicious. If I ask for a recipe, so familiar are the makers with the dishes that they often are vague and dependent on what is in the cupboards or larders at the time of making. So this is my version, I love it and love to share it too, and that is what matters really.

1 bag sev based snack (look in the world food aisle at your supermarket, sev are snacks made from gram flour)
Chutney
½ pack mini poppadoms
2 tbsp pomegranate seeds
Pomegranate molasses
Juice of ½ lime

○ You can make one large batch of this snack or make a small bowl at a time. The lime juice and molasses will soften the sev so if you prefer your snacks crunchy, small batches it is then.

○ Combine the sev and poppadoms together. Stir in the chutney, add a squeeze of lime, a drizzle of molasses and a sprinkle of pomegranate seeds.

Save it *Freeze the remaining pomegranate seeds for your gin and tonic.*

○ Sit, chat and share.

Cook's tip *You can buy pomegranate juice in ethnic stores as well as major supermarkets. Look for it in the 'international' aisle.*

Gin and tonic with pomegranate ice

No one, especially not me, needs an excuse to indulge in a gin and tonic. Leftover pomegranate seeds do often end up desiccating in the fridge, so why not put them to good use. Not only does the ice bejewel the gin and tonic beautifully but it may even count towards your five a day. Brilliant!

Makes 2 glasses

1 bottle good-quality gin (Bombay Sapphire for me)
1 bottle good-quality tonic (Fever tree is really lovely)
1 tbsp frozen pomegranate seeds

○ Using a wooden spoon handle, hit the pomegranate skin to dislodge the seeds. Try not to gouge them out if you can avoid it.

○ Place the seeds onto a tray and place into the freezer. Try to keep them separate if you can. Once frozen, slide into a bag and keep until the need for a G and T arises – about once every two days in my case.

○ Into a tall glass, tip a handful of ice and pour in 2 measures of gin.

○ Top up with four measures of tonic. Slide in the frozen pomegranate seeds. Stir once and serve.

○ Repeat as necessary.

Shopping list

3 carrots

3 celery sticks

2 onions

3 tomatoes

2kg piece of gammon

100ml double cream

2 tbsp orange juice

400g split peas

1 small jar peanut butter smooth or crunchy

From the storecupboard

Butter

Cloves

Eggs

Flour – strong white bread

Jam

Lard

Milk

Mustard

Oil – olive

Sugar – caster and soft dark brown

Vanilla powder or extract

Yeast – dried

Gammon chain

Surprising as it may seem, there are times when I have other things to do than be in the kitchen slaving over a hot stove. Baking fresh bread for the sandwiches may seem like a lot of effort and a bit of a contradiction then. It isn't a great deal of work, only short bursts of energy interspersed with periods of waiting.

As both bread and ham star in separately or together in all dishes, starting with the best you can is a good mantra to follow.

Boiled and baked gammon → use the cold ham and ham stock to make →
Pea and ham soup which is a meal in itself, but can also be served with →
Boiled and baked gammon → again using the cold ham, bake fresh bread to make →
Ham sandwiches with crusty bread → get full value from the bread and make →
PBJ pudding

Boiled and baked gammon

In this recipe, you boil the gammon to cook it, then bake a delicious, sweet glaze over the top. Do be careful of your fingers, when you are preparing it, though!

Serves 4

2kg piece of gammon (smoked or unsmoked)
1 onion, studded with 6 cloves
1 tsp whole black peppercorns
2 carrots, halved
2 celery sticks, halved
Water to cover
4 tbsp soft dark brown sugar
2 tbsp orange juice

To serve
Sweet potato mash
Green beans

○ Into a large, deep saucepan, place the piece of gammon, the vegetables and the spices. Fill the pan with enough water to just cover the gammon piece.

○ Bring the water slowly to the boil. When the water boils, turn the heat down, put a lid on the pan or tightly cover with foil and simmer. A gammon needs to cook for 20 minutes per 450g plus 20 minutes.

○ Once the gammon has finished cooking in the liquid, remove the gammon to a plate and cover.

Save it *Strain the cooking liquor into a large bowl and put into the fridge for use in the pea and ham soup. The vegetables can be discarded.*

○ Preheat the oven to 220°C/gas 7 and line a large roasting tin with foil. This is vital as the sugar and orange juice used to glaze the ham will become toffee as it heats up in the oven. Whoever does the washing up will hate you if you forget. If you are doing your own washing up, I am sure there will be no forgetfulness.

○ Using a sharp knife and asbestos fingers, remove the rind and some of the fat from the gammon joint. Score the remaining fat layer. You can use straight lines, a checkerboard pattern or create diamond shapes – it is up to you.

○ Mix together the sugar, orange juice and smear all over the top surface of the ham. Place into the oven and bake for 15 minutes until the sugar and juice mixture is bubbly and glossy. Allow to cool slightly, otherwise the hot sugar on top of the ham will necessitate a trip to A and E. Slice thickly and serve.

Save it *There will be plenty of ham left for tomorrow.*

○ Personal favourite accompaniments in this house are heaps of sweet potato mash and a bowl of squeaky green beans.

Pea and ham soup

Quite simply, pea and ham soup is a hug in a bowl. There are some, mostly my children, who don't think soup counts as a meal. I defy anyone to do anything more strenuous than read every page of a Saturday broadsheet having filled themselves up with this delicious and quite frankly rib-sticking concoction.

Serves 4

400g split peas
1 tbsp olive oil
½ onion, diced
1 celery stick, diced
1 carrot, diced
200g cooked ham, shredded or diced
1.5l ham stock – if you have more, keep it, you may find you need it!
Salt and freshly ground black pepper

○ Soak the split peas overnight in cold water. Discard any peas that fail to swell. Look carefully and discard any small pieces of grit you may find. Rinse well.

○ In a large pan, add a slug of olive oil, the onion, celery and carrot. Cook gently to soften the vegetables, caramelising a little to bring out their flavours.

○ Add the stock and the soaked split peas. Bring to the boil and simmer very gently for 1½–2 hours. If the soup appears to be thickening too much for your taste, then use a little more of the reserved stock or just plain water to thin the soup as you'd like.

○ Again it is up to you. If you like a chunky soup then you can leave the soup as it is. For a smooth soup or if you just want to hide the vegetables from the children, then use a hand blender or liquidiser and blitz away.

○ Serve in a warm bowl with a handful of the shredded ham scattered on top.

○ After eating, challenge the soup naysayers to a game of Swing ball in the garden. I am betting they will say no!

Cook's tip For me, a good soup is based on either a deeply flavoured well-made stock, a base of sweated vegetables or, in the case of this soup, both. The flavours need to be balanced and one should not overwhelm the other. To be honest I'd try to avoid the soups that suggest you empty the contents of your vegetable rack into a pan of water, heat it up and blend it. Yes, it will make you a soup but it might not satisfy your taste buds greatly. Pick pairs of flavours that work well: carrot and orange, spiced parsnip, broccoli and blue cheese and build upon that. Experiment and see. Have fun!

Ham sandwiches with crusty bread

Fresh bread rarely needs more than a slick of salty creamy butter to top it off to perfection. I always will play indigestion roulette with a freshly baked loaf, so much do I enjoy it. If you insist on adding more than butter to make a sandwich, then you can't go wrong with a thick slice of ham and possibly a tomato or a smear of hot English mustard. If you plan to make a doorstep filled with sausages or be dainty and serve wafer-thin cucumber sandwiches, then baking your own bread will enhance these delicacies no end.

Serves 4

For the crusty white bread
750g strong white flour, plus extra for dusting
25g butter or lard
2 tsp table salt
1 sachet dried yeast (usually about 7g)
2 tsp caster sugar
450ml warm water

For the filling
Butter
Slices of ham
Tomatoes, sliced
English mustard

Make the bread

○ Place the flour and butter in a large bowl. Rub the butter into the flour as you would for pastry. Stir in the salt, sugar and dried yeast.

○ Begin to add the water. You can use a mixer and a dough hook but your hands work just as well. Be brave, wet dough will rise much better than a dry one. Of course, dough should not be liquid but trust me!

○ Knead the dough on a well-floured surface. If using a dough hook in a mixer, 5 minutes mixing should produce smooth and elastic dough; using your hands you will need 10 minutes. You will, of course, be using up calories so can justify that extra slice of buttered fresh bread later!

○ Put in an oiled bowl, cover with oiled clingfilm and place to one side for 1–1½ hours to rise until doubled in size.

○ Knock back the dough. Think of a reason and punch the dough in the middle to deflate it – cheaper than counselling. Shape the dough as you want: use a lightly oiled loaf tin or shape onto a baking tin. Cover and leave for a further 30 minutes to rise again.

○ Preheat the oven to 230°C/gas 8.

○ Bake the loaf for 30–40 minutes. A loaf is baked when it sounds hollow when tapped on the bottom.

○ Leave to cool – I usually manage 10 minutes!

Make the sandwiches

○ Cut slices of the bread, but be careful as it will be soft and squishy. Butter, add a thick slice of ham, mustard to taste and relish your achievements.

PBJ pudding

One thing you can say about factory bread is that it seems to last for several days without going stale. I'm not sure this is a good thing necessarily. It is sad when bread you have made stales but there are a few compensations. Stale bread is a brilliant excuse to make some fantastic recipes. You can't make panzanella too often, and then there is bread and butter pudding. The combination of crispy exterior and slightly soufleed rich creamy interior is a textural workout for the mouth. Add peanut butter and jam and I may well have gone to heaven already!

Serves 4

8 slices of bread, crusts removed
Butter, softened
Peanut butter (chunky or smooth)
Jam (bramble or raspberry works best here)
100ml double cream
300ml whole milk
2 eggs
2 tbsp caster sugar
1 tsp vanilla powder or extract

- Generously butter a 1l pie dish.

- Butter the bread on both sides. This is a little messy but makes the finished pudding really crispy so it is worth the effort.

- Take each pair of bread slices and make a generously filled peanut butter and jam sandwich. Cut each sandwich into triangular quarters. Repeat with all the slices of bread. At the end you should have 16 small triangular PBJ sandwiches.

- Arrange the sandwiches in the buttered dish with the points of the triangle facing upwards.

- Preheat the oven to 180°C/gas 4.

- In a small saucepan, heat the cream and milk until just bubbling at the edges. In a separate bowl, whisk together the eggs, 1 tbsp of the caster sugar and the vanilla. Pour over the warmed milk and combine well.

- Return the egg and milk mixture to the saucepan and cook gently until the custard thickens and coats the back of a spoon. Pour over the PBJ sandwiches and press the sandwiches into the custard. If you can, leave the sandwich and custard mixture for half an hour to allow the bread to absorb as much of the custard as possible.

- Scatter over the remaining sugar. Pop into the oven for 30–35 minutes until golden and crispy.

- Serve with another dollop of jam on the side and cold, cold ice cream. Raspberry ripple would be good especially if you have used raspberry jam!

Shopping list

6 red peppers

Vegetables of your choice to accompany the roast pork

1.5kg boned and rolled pork shoulder

2 floury baps

1 pack quick-cook polenta or 1 pack ready-made polenta

2 tbsp grated Parmesan cheese

150g hazelnuts

From the storecupboard

Cocoa powder

Garlic clove

Oil - olive and vegetable

Sugar - icing

Vanilla powder or extract

Wine vinegar - red

Slow-roast pork shoulder chain

One of life's joys is stepping through the front door to be greeted warmly by the smell of dinner cooking gently in the oven. A slow-roast shoulder of pork fits this bill magnificently. The uplifting sensation given by the thought of dinner readying itself by melting and becoming tender and unctuous can be gone in a flash. Even if I am met at the door by a storm of requests, demands and disputes to solve, if there is a shoulder of pork slowly cooking away in the oven, I know I have much to look forward to.

Travelling along this slow-roast pork chain will provide you with dish after dish of deep rich flavours and textures.

Slow-roast pork shoulder → shred the pork, bathe it in the cooking juices, add rich roasted peppers, pop in a bap and make →
Pulled pork buns with roasted peppers → grill some polenta, use the peppers to make →
Grilled polenta with romesco sauce → finish the bag of hazelnuts by making →
Homemade nut and chocolate spread

Slow-roast pork shoulder

The juxtaposition of soft, gravy rich meat and the crisp shatter of the crackling is what really sends me back to the roasting tin for a second helping. You can't hurry a slow-roast pork shoulder so plan this meal for a cool Saturday evening. The bonus is the house gets heated by the oven too, without the battle of the thermostat having to commence.

Serves 4

1.5kg boned and rolled pork shoulder
100ml boiling water
Sea salt

To serve
Sugarsnap peas
Roasted carrots
Cauliflower cheese

○ Preheat the oven to 220°C/gas 7.

○ Take the joint out of any packaging and dry the crackling with a wad of kitchen towel. To make crisp crackling, the drier the pork skin the better.

○ Place the joint into a deep roasting tin and slam into the oven for 20 minutes to begin to crisp up the crackling.

○ After the first 20 minutes, turn the oven down to 160°C/gas 3 and cook for a further 2 hours and 40 minutes until the meat is tender.

○ Turn the oven back up to 240°C/gas 8.

○ Remove the meat from the oven and place on a warm plate. Carefully slide a sharp knife under the crackling layer and detach it from the pork underneath. Cover the meat with a layer of foil and leave to rest as you deal with the crackling.

○ Pop the crackling layer back onto a clean roasting dish and return to the oven for 15 minutes or so until the crackling is crisp and puffy. Check every 5 minutes or so as crackling can catch and burn easily.

○ Scrape any crusty bits from the bottom of the meat roasting pan and pour on the boiling water. Pour this meaty liquor into a jug. Drain any meat juices from the resting pork into the same jug.

Save it for the pulled pork buns recipe. Refrigerate until needed.

○ Shred any remaining pork into the juices whilst still warm. You may eat a few pieces as you go along – these are the cook's perks – but be warned, the more you eat now, the less there is left for tomorrow.

○ I love to serve roasted pork shoulder with a big bowl of sugar snap peas, roasted carrots and cauliflower cheese.

Pulled pork buns with roasted peppers

The combination of intensely savoury and richly sweet is a winner in my book. I'll happily eat sweet and salty popcorn in the cinema, salted caramel toffees in the car and maple syrup pancakes with bacon every time I cross over the Atlantic. Classically, pulled pork buns have an apple sauce accompaniment or perhaps sweet coleslaw to finish the sandwich. I love to have roasted peppers topping my pulled pork sandwich. Roasting the peppers enhances the sweetness no end. If you really can't do sweet and savoury together just have the gravy but you are missing a real treat. Go on, try it – you might surprise yourself!

Serves 2

6 peppers
2 large floury baps
400g shredded pork
Reserved cooking liquor
Vegetable oil
Olive oil
Salt and freshly ground black pepper

Roast the peppers

○ Preheat the oven to 220°C/gas 7 and lightly oil the baking tray.

○ Place the peppers onto the tray and slide the tray into the oven. Bake the peppers until the skin is charred and bubbled; this will take about 40 minutes but check after 30 to be on the safe side. Take the peppers from the oven.

○ Turn the oven down to 180°C/gas 4.

○ Lay the hot peppers into a bowl and cover with clingfilm to trap the steam. It is this steam that will make the pepper skin come away cleanly. Leave to cool a little.

Heat the pork

○ In a baking dish, place the cold shredded pork and moisten with the cooking juices reserved from yesterday. The pork needs some liquor to help it steam in the oven but doesn't need to poach so don't be too heavy handed. About 150ml should do it. Cover tightly with foil and bake in the oven for 20 minutes.

Finish the peppers and finish the dish

○ Now the peppers have cooled, rub off the charred skin and remove any seeds and membranes from inside. A little charring may remain and that will add to the smoky flavour of the final sandwich.

Save it *Keep two red peppers to one side for the romesco sauce later in the chain.*

○ Slice the remaining roasted peppers into a bowl and dress with a slug of olive oil and salt and pepper to taste.

○ Remove the pork from the oven once heated through.

○ Take a large floury bap, stuff as much pork and as many peppers into the bun as you think you can eat. Take a tea towel as a napkin and enjoy. This is messy and delicious.

Grilled polenta with romesco sauce

I am not a vegetarian: however, after two meals that are deeply meaty you do sometimes need to give your digestive tract a little bit of a rest. Polenta with romesco sauce is almost entirely protein-free. You can hardly count the few rasps of Parmesan as it really features in the dish for the intangible rich back note it delivers. If you cannot live without meat, then polenta and romesco sauce will pair very well with grilled chicken. It won't add to the washing up either as the grill pan used for the polenta can be used for the chicken too. Less washing up is always a good thing, I find.

Serves 4

For the polenta
1 pack of quick-cook polenta (about a 4–5 serving pack)
Boiling water
2 tbsp freshly grated Parmesan

For the romesco sauce
2 roasted red peppers, peeled and deseeded
1 tbsp hazelnuts (a real tbsp not a 15ml measure!)
1 garlic clove, peeled
1 tbsp olive oil
1 tbsp red wine vinegar

To serve
Green salad
Grilled chicken (optional)

Link it *I bought a 150g bag of nuts and saved the remainder for the nut and chocolate spread.*

Make the polenta

○ Line a 15 x 25cm tin with clingfilm.

○ Make up the polenta with boiling water as directed on the pack. At the end of the cooking time, beat the Parmesan into the polenta.

○ Pour the polenta into the lined tin, smooth the top and place on one side to cool a little before placing in the fridge.

Make the sauce

○ Place all the ingredients for the sauce into a food processor or use a hand blender. Blitz the ingredients until smooth and the sauce has taken on a paler creamy consistency. This will take just 30 seconds to a minute.

Cook the polenta

○ Put the chargrill pan on to heat up. If you don't have one, a dry frying pan will do, you just won't get the char lines.

○ Take the polenta from the fridge and tip it out from the tin onto a chopping board. Peel off the clingfilm. Take an oiled knife and cut 1.5–2cm slices.

○ Lay these slices into the hot pan and cook for 3–4 minutes each side, or until the char lines form and darken.

○ Serve hot with the cold romesco sauce, and a small green salad. If you really have to, a side of grilled chicken will do too!

Homemade nut and chocolate spread

So we have had the savoury and now for the sweet. Nut and chocolate spread is such a versatile ingredient. Simply spread on toast for breakfast it will keep everyone happy; used to fill a crêpe it is seriously indulgent. I have even used it as an emergency topping for cupcakes. Homemade chocolate hazelnut spread is so easy and tastes like heaven.

Makes 150g

125g hazelnuts
2 tbsp flavourless oil
2 tbsp icing sugar, sifted
1 tbsp cocoa powder
½ tsp vanilla powder or extract
A pinch of salt

○ Preheat the oven to 200°C/gas 6.

○ Spread the hazelnuts onto a flat baking tray and roast in the oven for 5 minutes. Check on them every couple of minutes as they are as wayward as an unattended toddler. Do not let them burn.

○ You can spend time removing all the skin from the hazelnuts if you want but I don't bother. Give them a rub in a sieve and get off what you can but really life is too short!

○ Allow to cool for about half an hour and then blitz in a food processor. This will take a few minutes, the nuts will go from whole, to dust and then to a thick paste. Keep going, have faith, the nut oil will be released and gradually an oily gloop will form.

○ To this gloop, add the other ingredients and blast the paste again. The mixture will thin and become glossy. Once completely blended together, taste and check for both flavour and texture. If you like your paste really smooth, keep processing; if you like a slightly chunkier paste, then stop.

○ Put on some toast, make a crêpe or just eat it out of the food processor bowl. I'm not telling.

Shopping list

1 lemon	Vermouth
4 large tomatoes or 400g can chopped tomatoes (for pie)	2 measures gin for every 1 measure vermouth
1 x 400g can chopped tomatoes (for gnocchi)	350g black or green olives
200g salad leaves	3 anchovies
2 onions	500g minced beef
1 fresh rosemary sprig	1.5kg potatoes for mashing
2.5kg leg of lamb	
500g new potatoes	
Whisky	
Grapefruit juice	
Maraschino cherry syrup	
Prune juice	

From the storecupboard

Baking powder	Lard or white vegetable fat
Butter	Milk
Chilli flakes	Oil – olive
Eggs	Oregano
Flour – plain	Stock
Garlic clove	

Butterflied leg of lamb chain

We all know that just because the sun shines one day it doesn't follow that the next day will be sunny too. Goodness me, you can say the same thing about morning and afternoons most days. Links in this lamb chain cater for that unpredictability in weather. Fill you up, hearty meals to please everyone, including the cook as the recipe for a dirty martini is here too. Remember too that if you have a barbecue there is no law that says you can't use it on colder days. Actually I love to barbecue on cold days, red wine in hand, warmth from the coals and smells to drive your neighbours to distraction. What's not to like!

Butterflied leg of lamb → use the lamb to make a proper →
Shepherd's pie → use the additional mashed potato to create →
Gnocchi with ragu → take a portion of the ragu for the filling in the →
Beef and olive empanadas → use a few remaining olives and a splash of the olive brine to make →
A dirty martini, a colonial cocktail or an old yeller

Butterflied leg of lamb

Succulently pink on the inside and darkly crisp on the outside, a butterflied leg of lamb looks magnificent on the barbecue. Marinated to infuse the meat with perfume and punch this lamb dish is a real family favourite. Don't panic about the anchovies, they melt to supply a salty savouriness to the dish that is a revelation to all. Ask your butcher to butterfly (remove the bone from) your leg of lamb. Although, it is perfectly possible to do this yourself with a steady hand, a boning knife and a quick look at YouTube.

Serves 4

1 2.5kg leg of lamb (weight with bone in)
1 garlic clove, cut into slivers
1 rosemary sprig, leaves stripped and stems discarded
3 tinned anchovies, finely chopped
Olive oil
Grated zest of 1 lemon
Salt and freshly ground black pepper

To serve
Boiled new potatoes
Leafy green salad
Lemon wedges

○ Preheat the oven to 180°C/gas 4 or get the barbecue coals going.

○ Take a sharp knife and poke holes all over the skin side of the lamb. Into these holes, poke pieces of garlic, anchovy and rosemary.

○ Take 1 tbsp of olive oil and mix this with the lemon zest. Rub all over the lamb. Season well with pepper and a little salt. The anchovies are salty so take care here.

○ If cooking in the oven, roast for 50 minutes for very pink to 1hr 10 minutes for medium roasted lamb. Leave to rest for 10 minutes.

○ If using the barbecue, put on your coat and put up the umbrella. Push the coals to one side as you need an indirect heat for cooking large pieces of meat on the barbecue. Place the lamb on the side away from the coals and cook for 50 minutes to just over an hour. Turn regularly.

○ Carve and serve two-thirds of the meat family style on a big platter with a big bowl of hot buttery new potatoes and a leafy green salad. Tuck some lemon wedges around the lamb and spritz the meat as you eat.

Save it *Save the remaining meat for the shepherd's pie.*

Shepherd's pie

I have memories of standing in a kitchen, helping to mince the leftover meat from Sunday's roast. I have no idea if it was beef or lamb but I do recall the mincer was blue. You don't need a mincer here, but you will need leftover lamb. If it's beef you have, you're making a cottage pie, but the recipe remains basically the same so don't fret. It stands to reason that shepherd's pie is made with lamb, although if you want to tell other people's children that it is made from real shepherds, please feel free.

Serves 4

2 tbsp oil
1 onion, finely chopped
500g lamb, finely diced or minced if you have the technology
4 large tomatoes, skinned and deseeded or 400g can chopped tomatoes
300ml chicken stock
A splash of wine (optional)
1.5kg mashing potatoes, peeled and cut into chunks
Butter
Milk
Salt and freshly ground black pepper

To serve
Peas
Carrots
Gravy

Make the filling
○ Preheat the oven to 200°C/gas 6.

○ Heat half the oil in a pan and add the onion. Stir to coat and cook gently until softened but not coloured.

○ Add the minced lamb. Cook the lamb until heated through and the dice have broken up a little. Keep the meat moving and break up any large lumps with your wooden spoon.

○ Add the tomatoes to the meat in the pan. Slosh in the stock to cover. A splash of wine wouldn't go amiss here if you have some knocking around. Stir to loosen the stickiness on the bottom of the pan. Bring up to a simmer, then reduce the heat until the surface of the meat just shivers. Cover and leave for at least 30 minutes, stirring occasionally.

Cook the potatoes

○ With about 20 minutes to go, put the potatoes on to boil in well-salted water. Cutting the potatoes up small will help speed up the cooking process. When cooked through, drain well and leave in a colander over the warm pan to dry out a little.

○ If you have a potato ricer, please use as it virtually guarantees lump-free mash. If you don't have one, get online and order one. Meanwhile enlist child labour and get them to mash the potato for you.

Finish the pie

○ After about 30 minutes, the stock should have reduced to thickish gravy and the meat should be very tender. If the gravy isn't as thick as you want it, raise the temperature and reduce the sauce down further. Check for seasoning.

○ Pour the meat into a baking dish and top with two-thirds of the potatoes. Rough up the potato topping so that it gets those crispy edges everyone fights over (or is that just my house?). Dot the top of the shepherd's pie with butter. Bake for 25 minutes or until the topping is golden and bubbly.

Save it Keep the remaining potato for the gnocchi later in the week.

○ Serve with a big bowl of peas, some baby carrots and lots of gravy.

Gnocchi with ragu

Sitting in a small fisherman's café on an island in the Bay of Naples, I was first introduced to gnocchi. On that day, mine were drenched in a simple tomato sauce and shavings of Parmesan. I love these little pillows of potato. Soft and a little chewy, they ring the changes from pasta or rice. A foil for many sauces, one of my absolute favourites is a slowly cooked ragu.

Serves 4

For the ragu
1 onion, finely chopped
2 garlic cloves, crushed
500g lean beef mince
400g can chopped tomatoes
1 tbsp chopped fresh oregano or 1 tsp dried
A pinch of chilli flakes
150ml stock

For the gnocchi
500g cold mashed or riced potatoes
175–200g plain flour, plus extra for dusting
1 egg, beaten
Salt and freshly ground black pepper

To serve
Butter
Olive oil
Parmesan

Make the ragu

○ Brown the onions in a saucepan and then add the garlic. Garlic has a higher sugar content so needs to be cooked for a shorter time than the onion. Slide in the minced beef and cook until well browned. Keep the meat moving in the pan to break up any lumps. Stir in the tinned tomatoes, herbs and chilli flakes.

○ Pour in the stock and combine well together. Bring to the simmer, then reduce the heat until the surface of the mince mixture just quivers. Leave to cook until the ragu is thick and glossy. This will take up to an hour on a very low heat.

Make the gnocchi

○ Preheat the oven to 200°C/gas 6.

○ Meanwhile make the gnocchi. Put all the gnocchi ingredients into a large bowl. Use your hands – easier to find and clean than trying to assemble a mixer – and work the ingredients together to form a dough.

○ Flour the work surface and your hands. Take balls of dough and roll them out into sausages about 1.5–2cm. thick. Cut into lengths of again 2cm. Using the back of fork prongs, dent each piece of dough gently. This makes them look pretty and gives the sauce something to cling to.

○ Bring a large pan of salted water to the boil. Drop batches of gnocchi into the pan. When they rise to the surface, after a few minutes, they are cooked. Drain and place in a buttered dish. When all the gnocchi are cooked, dot with a little more butter. Shave some Parmesan over the top and bake for 10 minutes.

○ When baked, pour three-quarters of the sauce over the gnocchi and plonk in the middle of the table. Call the rest of the family to come and eat. The last one to the table gets the least.

Save it Keep the remaining sauce for use in the empanadas later or freeze in a container for another day.

Beef and olive empanadas

My mother always said you should not eat food out on the street. 'Sit at the table and use proper cutlery, please.' Eating on the go is not really to be recommended but sometimes cannot be avoided. Empanadas make a delicious addition to a lunch box and since you have to sit to eat them as the pastry is very flaky, my mum would be pleased with them too.

Makes 8

For the pastry dough
400g plain flour
1 tsp baking powder
1 tsp salt
50g butter
50g lard or white vegetable fat
1 egg, lightly beaten
Water at room temperature
1 portion of ragu
12 green olives (or black if you prefer), cut into rings

○ Preheat the oven to 180°C/gas 4.

○ Sift the flour into a large bowl with the baking powder and the salt. Rub in the butter and lard until the mixture resembles breadcrumbs. Using a round-ended knife, stir in the water until the dough begins to come together. Use your hands to gently form a ball of dough.

○ Wrap the dough in clingfilm and refrigerate for 30 minutes to allow the dough to rest. Make a cup of tea and relax.

○ Roll out the dough to about 3mm thick and cut out 8 circles about 10cm in diameter. I usually find a saucer helps me to do this.

○ Whisk together the egg and a tablespoon of water.

○ Stir the olives into the ragu. Place about a dessertspoon of the ragu in the middle of each dough circle. Moisten the edge of the circle and press together. Using a fork, crimp the edges together to seal. Very pretty too. Brush with more egg wash.

○ Bake in the oven for 10–12 minutes until golden and crisp. Wash down with the following recipe.

Dirty martini

Winston Churchill famously liked his martinis so dry he simply left the open bottle of vermouth next to the poured gin. I like mine less so but then I don't much care for cigars either!

Makes 2

2 measures gin
Anything from 2 drops to 1 measure vermouth
1–2 tbsp olive juice from the jar
Ice
2 olives

○ Whizz the gin, vermouth and olive juice in a blender, then serve over ice with an olive to garnish.

Colonial cocktail

If you still have olives left over, then you can also indulge in a colonial cocktail, which basically works on a 2:1 ratio.

Makes 2

2 measures gin
1 measure grapefruit juice
A splash of maraschino cherry syrup
2 olives
Ice

○ Whizz the gin, grapefruit and cherry syrup in a blender, then serve over ice with an olive to garnish.

Old yeller

Another unusual cocktail that will use up those olives.

Makes 2

2 measures whisky
2 measures prune juice
2 olives
Ice
A twist of lemon

○ Whizz the whisky, prune juice and olives in a blender, then serve over ice with a twist of lemon to garnish.

Shopping list

2 limes
1 green chilli
2 carrots
1 celery stick
1 bunch spring onions
3 onions
200g small or cherry tomatoes
1 small bunch fresh coriander
2kg boned and rolled beef brisket
150ml soured cream
Tomato salsa, optional
Guacamole, optional
12 taco shells

From the storecupboard

Chilli flakes	Peas - frozen
Chocolate - dark	Rice - basmati
Egg	Soy sauce
Garlic cloves	Stock
Horseradish sauce	Tomato purée
Oil - olive, sesame and vegetable	Wine - red

Beef pot roast chain

As those who know me can vouch, I am built for comfort and not for speed, so doing things slowly comes easily to me. I have recently taken to slowly roasting those slightly old-fashioned cuts of meat such as pork belly, brisket and lamb shoulder for the whole of a Sunday afternoon and I am finding not only is the food bill cheaper for the Sunday dinner, as these cuts are less expensive, but the house smells magnificent so my Yankee Candle bill is lower too. The brisket has to be my favourite at the moment and it leads to so many other delicious dishes too.

The keynote flavour has to be the deep, rich umami taste derived from the roasting meats. One large piece of brisket, slowly roasted, passes on a density of almost marmite richness to all the dishes in this chain.

Beef pot roast → use the stock and braised vegetables along with some tomatoes to make →
Roasted beef and tomato soup →
Beef pot roast → use the remaining brisket to make →
Beef tacos and Mexican rice → use the rice to make →
Egg fried rice

Beef pot roast

If you have to spend the morning standing on a touchline, and the afternoon scraping the mud off someone else's muddy boots, then you really don't want to spend the evening cooking a roast dinner. A slow-roasted beef brisket may be the answer, but don't let anyone else know how easy this pot roast is though otherwise I can guarantee they will find something for you to do! Brisket is happy served with traditional roasted vegetables and a Yorkshire pudding, big fluffy baked potatoes and coleslaw, or inside a floury bap with loads of hot mustard. Just serve it!

Serves 4

2 onions, halved and sliced
2kg piece of boned and rolled brisket
Salt and freshly ground black pepper
2 carrots, chopped into sticks
1 celery stick, cut into batons
2 garlic cloves, bruised
1l stock, made from a combination of fresh stock, stock cubes, red wine or just water

To serve
Baked potatoes
Yorkshire pudding
Roasted vegetables
Coleslaw

○ Heat the oven to 225°C/gas 7.

○ Lay the onions in the bottom of a lidded casserole dish or a deep baking tray. Season the brisket all over with plenty of salt and pepper. Pop this onto the onion base and blast in the hot oven for 20–25 minutes to render the fat cap down and give the meat some colour.

○ Remove the joint from the oven, turn the oven down to 150°C/gas 2, add the carrots, celery and garlic, and pour the stock around the beef. Cover the roasting dish tightly with the lid or a double layer of foil and put the whole lot back in the oven. For posher occasions, I have used a can of beef consommé as the base for the stock.

○ Every hour, remove the foil, baste the joint and top up the stock level with water, but more red wine would be magnificent too.

○ Cook for at least another 3 hours. Your house will soon start to smell fabulous. Any teenage boys need to be sent out to play football at this point. If not, they will eat all the biscuits in the house whilst waiting for this brisket to cook.

○ Remove the meat from the stock and allow it to rest for 20 minutes somewhere warm.

Save it *Keep the stock and the braised vegetables as they are needed for the next link in the chain.*

○ Serve the meat with baked potatoes, Yorkshire pudding, roasted vegetables and coleslaw.

Save it *Any remaining meat will be used tomorrow.*

Roasted beef and tomato soup

When I was younger I'd often get to choose the soup we'd have for Saturday lunch. As this was the 1970s, the soup would almost certainly have been condensed in a tin or dehydrated in a packet. If I was choosing tinned I have cream of asparagus, and packet was always oxtail. Pretty peculiar choices for a six-year-old, looking back now, but then that's me all over, I suppose. Roasted beef and tomato soup took me back to the rich, meaty flavour of the oxtail soup. In this case, it's the roasted tomatoes that give the deep umami flavour and not the chemicals so beloved of food producers in the 70s.

Serves 2 greedy people or 4 as a snack with the addition of a sandwich

200g small or cherry tomatoes
2 garlic cloves
2 tbsp olive oil
Salt and freshly ground black pepper
1l stock and braised vegetables from the pot roast

To serve
Horseradish cream (optional)

○ Preheat the oven to 200°C/gas 6.

○ Lay the tomatoes on a baking tray with the unpeeled garlic cloves. Drizzle with a little olive oil, a good pinch of sea salt and a grind or two of black pepper. Pop into the oven for 25–30 minutes until soft and just oozing juice.

○ Take the cooled stock and braised vegetables from the fridge and skim off and discard any fat from the top of the stock. Pour the stock and vegetables into a large saucepan.

○ Place the tomatoes in boiling water for a few seconds, then in cold water, then peel off the skins. Add to the stock and vegetable mixture with the garlic.

○ Warm the ingredients together just to take the chill off and return the stock to a liquid state, if it has jellified.

○ Whizz the soup to a smooth state using a hand blender or a liquidiser. If the soup has warmed too much, allow to cool a touch before doing this as the hot liquid has a tendency to explode, usually landing on exposed and soft flesh – i.e. mine!

○ Once smooth, reheat the soup, making sure it doesn't boil. Serve with a chunk of bread and a swirl of horseradish cream, if you like.

Beef tacos with Mexican rice

Heavens above, you spend the first part of a child's life teaching them how to use cutlery, then you introduce them to all manner of exciting foods they can eat with their hands! One absolute favourite has to be tacos. The fact tacos can be customised to suit even the pickiest of individuals makes this a meal that all can enjoy and make their own. My version is pretty spicy, because we like it this way but please feel free to tone down the heat to meet your needs. The tacos can be made with minced beef, leftover chicken pieces taken from the bone or slow cooked pork shoulder pieces as well. Don't think I've made a mistake, the chocolate is there for a reason – try this recipe and see!

Serves 4

For the Mexican rice
1 tbsp vegetable oil
1 onion, chopped
2 garlic cloves, crushed
1 green chilli, finely chopped (if you feel brave, 2 chillies)
300g long-grain rice, such as basmati
600ml chicken or vegetable stock
Juice and grated zest of 2 limes

For the beef
A drizzle of oil
300g cooked beef brisket from the pot roast, cut into small chunks
1 tsp chilli flakes
2 tbsp tomato purée
2 squares dark chocolate
100ml water

To serve
Soured cream
Guacamole
Salsa
Grated cheese
Coriander
12 taco shells

Make the rice

○ Heat the oil in a large saucepan and fry the onion until soft, then stir in the crushed garlic and chilli for 1 minute.

○ Stir in the uncooked rice and get all the grains covered with the oil, onion and garlic.

○ Pour in the stock and lime juice, stir again and bring up to a simmer. Once simmering, cover tightly with a lid, turn off the heat and leave to steam for 15 minutes.

○ Remove the lid, fork through the rice to separate the grains and scatter artfully with the lime zest.

Save it Keep some rice back for the egg fried rice later in the week.

Make the tacos

○ Once the rice is steaming, turn your attention to the tacos. Heat a frying pan and add just a drizzle of oil. Toss in the cooked brisket and begin to warm through.

○ Add the tomato purée and cook for a moment. Now tip in the chilli flakes and combine well. Grate the squares of chocolate over the meat, add the water and cook very gently for about 20 minutes until all the water has evaporated. The meat will fall apart and no longer be chunks but this is perfectly fine, in fact it's brilliant! Turn off the heat and keep warm.

○ Place all the elements in bowls in the middle of the table and then insist everyone washes their hands. Encourage everyone to try different combinations of beef filling, guacamole, soured cream and salsa in their taco shell.

Vary it This works perfectly well with minced beef, leftover chicken pieces taken from the bone and slow-roasted pork shoulder too.

Egg fried rice

This was my absolute student standby, lunch, dinner and sometimes even breakfast when there were no Coco Pops in my cupboard! About time I passed it on to others. I make it still, only now with more care and sometimes a few more ingredients. Nothing wrong with only adding peas to your rice but it is possible to be oh so much more creative. If you haven't kept any of the Mexican rice, just use plain boiled rice.

Serves 1

1 egg
2 tsp sesame oil
1 tbsp vegetable oil
2 spring onions, thinly sliced
1 cup of frozen peas
A handful of cooked beef, cut into slivers
1 bowl cold cooked rice per person

To serve
Soy sauce

○ Whisk together the egg and the sesame oil; pop this on the side within reach.

○ Heat the vegetable oil in a wok or large saucepan until good and hot, quickly toss in the spring onions and then tip in the rice. Keep the pan contents moving. I find a wooden spoon is best for this but if you want to pretend to be Ken Hom and flick the rice out of the wok then be my guest – after all you are the one washing your own kitchen floor.

○ Now add the other softer vegetables and cooked meats. You only need to heat these through not cook them so this will only take a moment.

○ Finally whisk the egg, again using a fork or chopsticks, and drizzle in the rice, stirring as you go. The heat of the rice will cook the egg almost instantly.

○ Slide into a bowl, add a splash of soy sauce and enjoy.

If my children are reading this, I meant it about washing the kitchen floor!

Cook's tip *You could also add beansprouts, chopped water chestnuts, cashew nuts, prawns, and chopped ham, cold chopped chicken, chilli, whatever needs to be used up that is in your fridge – you are eating it!*

Shopping list

2 large brown onions

1 large Spanish onion

6 large baking potatoes

A bunch of fresh chives

900g sausages

500g minced beef

8 streaky bacon rashers

4 steaks

150g strong Cheddar cheese

300ml double cream

300ml soured cream

From the storecupboard

Butter

Eggs

Mustard - wholegrain

Oil - olive

Sugar - granulated

Wine - white

Wine vinegar - white

Steak haché and onions chain

I have already admitted to being a card-carrying carnivore. I apologise now if you prefer white meat to red or are happiest when getting your proteins from pulses but I love red meat. More than that I'm afraid (and the more sensitive amongst you may need to cover your eyes). I love a really tender and very rare steak. Not quite still mooing but as near as!

Steak just loves a potato too, and it is these versatile tubers that join the dishes in the steak and onions chain together.

Steak haché and onions with mustard sauce → use the reserved mustard sauce to enrich the mash for →
Sausages and mustard baked potato mash → take the cleaned out potato skins and make →
Stuffed potato skins
→ use a portion of the baked potato mash to fill a →
Span(ish) tortilla

Steak haché and onions with mustard sauce

Fret not. Steak haché is simply a posh burger. The mustard sauce will work very well with chicken breast too, although I'd sweeten it with a squirt of honey just before serving. Chips are the only carbohydrate that you could possibly consider serving with this meal.

Serves 4

For the onions
1 tbsp olive oil
A knob of butter
2 large brown onions, thinly sliced
1 tsp sugar
2 tsp white wine vinegar

For the steak
500g steak mince
Salt and freshly ground black pepper
1 tbsp oil

For the mustard sauce
1 small glass white wine
300ml double cream
1 tbsp wholegrain mustard
Juices from the resting steaks

To serve
Chunky chips
Watercress salad

Make the onions

○ The onions will take at least 30 minutes of slow and low cooking to get to the melting sweetness that makes them a vital component of this steak dish.

○ In a large saucepan, melt the oil and knob of butter over a high heat. Tip in the thinly sliced onions. Cook over a high heat until the onions just begin to caramelise, then turn the hob as low as it will go and leave to cook gently for 15 minutes.

○ Much of the liquid from the onions should have evaporated by now so add the sugar and vinegar. Cook for a further 15 minutes until golden brown and sticky.

Make the steak haché

○ Pop the mince into a bowl and season well with salt and pepper. Divide into quarters and shape each quarter into a patty.

○ Take a large, heavy-based frying pan, put on a medium heat and allow to get good and hot but not quite smoking.

○ Put a swirl or two of oil into the pan, enough to coat the base of the pan without any depth of oil remaining. Lay the burgers in the pan. Cook slowly until cooked through. If you like your burgers on the rare side, you need to buy freshly minced beef rather than any that is pre-prepared.

Make the mustard sauce

○ Deglaze the frying pan with the white wine, using a wooden spoon to scrape the sticky marmitey bits from the base of the pan as these make for a flavourful sauce. Boil to reduce by a third to a half.

○ Tip in the cream, mustard and burger juices, taste and season with salt and pepper.

Save it *Keep about half of the sauce for tomorrow's mashed potato.*

○ Serve the steak haché with chunky chips, a spoon of the caramelised onions with a couple of spoonfuls of the sauce over the top. A peppery watercress salad would be good with these burgers too.

Sausages and mustard baked potato mash

Sausages and mustard mash is one of those dishes you can pop in the oven and forget about. On those cold, drizzly, manic days when everyone in the family has to be at different places at the same time, sausage and baked potato mash helps feed everyone heartily with a minimum of fuss.

Serves 4

6 large baking potatoes, scrubbed
Olive oil
Sea salt
900g sausages (as many as your family will consume, which is 4 each in this house, but you may be more or less gluttonous than us!)
150ml mustard cream sauce
1 heaped tsp wholegrain mustard
A large knob of butter
Salt and freshly ground black pepper

To serve
Brown sauce or ketchup

Cook the potatoes and sausages
○ Preheat the oven to 200°C/gas 6.

○ Rub the potatoes all over with olive oil, then sprinkle each one with sea salt. Take a fork and prick the potatoes several times all over. This will prevent them from bursting out of their skin as they cook. Place on a baking tray and pop in the oven for 1½ hours. Once cooked, remove from the oven and allow to cool a little while you sort out the sausages.

○ Lay the sausages on a wire rack over a baking tray. Cook for 20 minutes; turn half way through to allow the sausages to brown on all sides.

Make the mash

○ Whilst the sausages are cooking, turn your attention to the mash. Cut each potato in half lengthways. Carefully scrape the fluffy, white interior into a heatproof bowl. If you feel the need, you can use a masher to take out any lumps from the mash.

Save it Place the potato skins into a lidded container and either place in the fridge for later or freeze for another day. Also keep to one side about two potatoes worth of mash for the Spanish tortilla. If you don't fancy making the tortilla, then simply eat more mash with your sausages!

○ Stir in the reserved mustard cream from yesterday, the mustard, a large knob of butter and salt and pepper to taste. If you would like more mustard or even butter or cream, now is the time to add this.

○ Serve a huge dollop of mash with the oven-baked sausages. I like brown sauce with my sausages. If you want ketchup you'll have to provide your own!

Stuffed potato skins

You should have 12 potato skin halves left from the previous recipe. You can use this recipe as a lunch for two, as a way to stave off hunger in several teenagers, or simply as part of a snack tea. I'm giving this as a very classic version of the recipe. Please customise it to your own personal likes and preferences. I'll put a few ideas at the end but I am sure you can come up with more twists on this recipe than me.

Serves 4

12 potato skin halves
Olive oil
8 streaky bacon rashers
150g strong Cheddar cheese, grated
Freshly ground black pepper
150ml soured cream
A few snipped fresh chives

To serve
A glass of cold beer

○ Take a large baking tray and place a wire tray on the top.

○ Using a pastry brush, brush a little oil on the potato skins inside and out. Place on the wire rack and place the bacon alongside. This is no time to be using lovely, thick rashers of back bacon. You want the bacon to be crisp to the point of crumbliness at the end of the cooking time.

○ Bake for 10–15 minutes until the edges of the skins are golden and crispy. The bacon should also be crisp and smelling wonderful.

○ Remove the skins from the oven, leaving the oven on. Divide the grated cheese evenly between the potato skins. Give a grind or two of black pepper. The skins should not need any salt as the cheese and bacon are probably salty enough. Scissor over the bacon, pop back in the oven and bake for a further 5 minutes until the cheese is melted and gooey.

○ Serve with a spoon of soured cream and a snip of chives. And a beer!

Vary it There are myriad variations to this dish. Blue cheese and pear, ricotta and pickled peppers, mozzarella and tomato, cheese and marmite . . . the list goes on. Experiment with flavour combinations you love – you are eating it and no critic is watching you. If the mixture of Cheddar and strawberry jam makes your mouth water, that's fine by me.

Spanish tortilla

I know very well that a proper Spanish tortilla needs to be made with raw potatoes, but as you know by now I don't have these, only some leftover mash. So I'm going to use that and make a Span(ish) omelette instead. If starting from scratch without the mash, just substitute 500g sliced new potatoes.

Serves 2

100ml olive oil
1 large white, preferably Spanish, onion, thinly sliced
Cold leftover mashed potato from two baking potatoes
4 eggs, broken up but not too well beaten
Salt and freshly ground black pepper

To serve
Ice-cold Spanish beer
Green salad or vegetable

○ Pour the oil into a high-sided, heavy-based frying pan (mine is 24cm across at the top). Slide in the onion and cook gently for 15 minutes. The onions should stew and not brown.

○ Now plop spoonfuls of the potato into the pan and cook for a further 15 minutes. The heat of the oil should set the potato but again not brown it at all.

○ In a bowl, although I often use a mug as the cupboard is closer, break up the eggs but don't whisk them too well. Season with salt and pepper.

○ Stir the seasoned eggs into the potato and onion mixture. Cook gently over a low heat until the eggs are set.

○ Place a plate over the cooked omelette and invert the plate and pan together. Allow to cool for a short while, cut into wedges and serve. An ice-cold Spanish beer is a great accompaniment. Add something green if you must.

Vary it *You can use this Span(ish) omelette recipe as a vehicle to use up other leftovers. Veggies such as pepper, broccoli or mushrooms can be slipped in with the egg. Chunks of ham and pieces of cooked spicy chorizo is another option. The beer is non-negotiable, though.*

Shopping list

2 large cooking apples, such as Bramley

1 small aubergine

½ butternut squash

1 carrot

2 courgettes

1 lemon

125g mushrooms

1 onion

1 red onion

1 yellow or orange pepper

4 pork loin steaks

From the storecupboard

Butter	Oil – olive
Cinnamon – ground	Parsley – fresh
Eggs	Rice – basmati
Flour – plain and strong bread	Stock
Garlic cloves	Sugar – caster and granulated
Lard or white vegetable shortening	Vanilla powder or extract
Milk	Yeast – dried

Roasted vegetable pilaf chain

When the evenings close in, or perhaps just when it is a wet Saturday in May, comfort food is guaranteed to make everyone feel better. Each link in this chain will warm the cockles of anyone's heart and possibly get the cook a hug of thanks into the bargain.

Roasted vegetable pilaf → use a portion to make →
Garlicky lemon and rice soup with homemade pitta breads → use a pitta to make breadcrumbs to cover →
Pork escalope with apple sauce → use the sauce to fill →
Apple and cinnamon doughnuts

Roasted vegetable pilaf

Whisper this quietly, but when you eat roasted vegetable pilaf, you really don't miss the meat at all. With so many textures and flavours holding a party on your taste buds, the vegetarian option is more than sufficient. By roasting the vegetables, it adds a depth of flavour that enhances and sweetens them. A smoky note also infuses the rice to give a subtle extra something to this dish.

Serves 4–5

1 red onion, quartered and sliced
1 yellow or orange pepper, quartered and sliced
1 carrot, chopped
2 courgettes, chopped
½ butternut squash, peeled and chopped
4 garlic cloves
1 small aubergine, chopped
125g mushrooms, wiped and chopped
4 tbsp olive oil
Sea salt and freshly ground black pepper
250g basmati rice
1l stock – vegetable, chicken, homemade or cube, it really doesn't matter

To serve
Green salad

○ Preheat the oven to 220°C/gas 7.

○ Into a large, deep casserole dish place the vegetables and the olive oil. Sprinkle with salt and pepper. Toss together and roast, uncovered, for 15 minutes until the vegetables just begin to colour a little.

○ Remove the tray from the oven, stir in the rice and stock. Cover, place back in the oven for 20 minutes, stirring occasionally.

○ Serve in a deep bowl with a crisp green salad and wait for your hug!

Save it Put a couple of portions in the fridge for tomorrow's dish.

Cook's tip If you don't have all the suggested vegetables but have a slightly different mixture – perhaps with tomatoes, sweet potatoes or maybe even asparagus – then please feel free to substitute them. Roasted vegetable pilaf is a great way to clear out the vegetable drawer in your fridge. Word of warning, salad mix doesn't roast well! A bunch of spring onions also works well in this dish instead of the onion.

Garlicky lemon and rice soup with homemade pitta breads

Soup should be hearty but it doesn't have to be chunky. Garlicky lemon and rice soup will warm you up from the tip of your toes to the very follicles on the top of your head. The rice makes the soup creamy and the pittas will give you a chance to scoop out the last morsel of deliciousness without sticking your head in the bowl to lick it out.

Serves 4

For the pitta bread
180g strong bread flour, plus extra for dusting
1 tsp salt
½ tbsp sugar
1 tsp fast-action dried yeast
1 tbsp olive oil
150–180ml water, at room temperature

For the soup
A knob of butter
1 tbsp olive oil
1 onion, finely chopped
4 garlic cloves, crushed.
1.5l chicken stock
Juice and grated zest of 1 lemon
2 servings of roasted vegetable pilaf, vegetables removed but kept to one side
Salt and freshly ground black pepper

Make the pittas

○ Place all the dry ingredients, including the yeast, in a large bowl and stir together. Add the olive oil and the water. Bring the dough together and then knead for 10 minutes until the dough is elastic.

○ Place in a clean, oiled bowl, cover with a clean tea towel and leave until doubled in size. This will take up to 2 hours on a cool day.

○ Divide the dough into 12 equal balls and leave to rise for about 30 minutes.

○ Preheat the oven to 220°C/gas 7 and place a lightly oiled baking sheet in the oven to heat up.

○ Roll out each ball of dough until thin. Quickly open the oven door and pop the dough onto the preheated sheet. Cook for 3–4 minutes until puffed and a little golden. Repeat until you have cooked all the pittas.

Make the soup

○ Melt together the butter and oil in a deep saucepan. Add the onions and cook gently for 5 minutes until softened but not coloured. Now add the garlic and cook again very gently for another 5 minutes.

○ Pour in the stock, lemon juice and lemon zest. At this point, add the roasted vegetables leftover from yesterday's pilaf, but not the cooked rice yet.

○ If you like a smoother soup, you can blitz the soup now with a hand blender. If you like chunky soup or just can't be faffed with washing up a blender, then chunky soup is fine too.

○ Taste and season with salt and black pepper. Tip in the cooked rice, stir and heat until piping hot.

○ Serve with your homemade pittas.

Save it Leftover pittas can be frozen for another meal.

Pork escalope with apple sauce

I do love crackling. There are times when provided with a roast pork dinner, the first thing I go for is the crispy, crunchy golden pork rind. Don't get me wrong, I love a succulent slice of the roasted pork too but crackling is not to be shared. It is the crisp outer layer on the pork escalope that helps to make this dish a favourite of mine. That, and the sweet and savoury combination of apple sauce and salty meat juices, of course.

Serves 4

For the apple sauce
2 large cooking apples, such as Bramleys, peeled, cored and chopped
2 tbsp caster sugar
A large knob butter
2 tbsp water

For the pork
4 pork loin steaks, fat removed
1 pitta bread, whizzed or grated to make breadcrumbs
1 tbsp chopped fresh parsley
4 tbsp plain flour
1 egg, beaten
Salt and freshly ground black pepper
A pinch of smoked paprika (optional)
Vegetable oil, for shallow frying

To serve
Mashed potatoes
Gravy

Make the apple sauce

○ Put all the apple sauce ingredients into a small saucepan. Place over a low heat and allow to stew down until soft and pulpy. Stir occasionally to prevent the sauce from catching on the bottom of the pan.

Save it *You'll need some apples for the next recipe so keep the sauce in the fridge.*

Cook the pork

○ Take a pork loin steak and place between two sheets of greaseproof paper. Using a rolling pin, beat the steak out until about 1cm thick. Place to one side and repeat with the rest of the pork loins.

○ Mix together the breadcrumbs and parsley.

○ Place the beaten egg, flour and breadcrumbs in separate bowls. Dip the pork into first the flour, then the eggs and then the breadcrumbs, keeping one hand for the wet ingredients and one for the dry. Set aside and repeat for the remaining escalopes.

○ Heat the oil in a shallow pan and fry the escalope until golden on one side. Turn the escalope over and cook on the other side.

○ Drain on kitchen paper. Serve with a huge pile of mashed potato, a dollop of apple sauce and lashings of salty gravy. Mmmmmm.

Apple and cinnamon doughnuts

Even when the cold wind on Brighton pier has penetrated my bones, a bag of hot doughnuts will warm me up. Doughnuts, fresh from the fryer, are made to be eaten on cold days. Slightly too hot to handle and covered in sparkling sugar crystals, doughnuts revive a jaded spirit instantly. Apple and cinnamon doughnuts are a little more sophisticated, but not much. I bet you can't eat one without licking your lips – go on I dare you.

Serves 4

180ml warm milk
60ml warm water
2 tsp dried yeast
75g caster sugar
425g plain flour, plus extra for dusting
½ tsp salt
1 tbsp lard or butter
1 egg
1 tsp vanilla powder or extract
Apple sauce left from the pork escalope
1 tsp ground cinnamon

○ Pour the milk into a small saucepan and warm through until it becomes lukewarm. Tip this into a jug and add the warm water, from the kettle will do, and stir in 1 tbsp of the sugar. Whisk in the dried yeast and leave for 10 minutes or so for the yeast to activate.

○ Sift the flour into the large bowl of your kitchen mixer, if you have one, and add the salt. Rub in the butter or lard. If you don't have a mixer, that's fine but be prepared to get your hands messy. Add the remaining sugar.

- Once the yeast has activated and left foam on the surface of the liquid, whisk the egg and vanilla into this yeasty mixture.

- Attach a dough hook to your mixer; pour the liquids onto the dry ingredients and leave to combine for 2–3 minutes. If you are using your hands, make a claw shape with your hand and combine the ingredients using a circular movement. Once amalgamated, you will need to continue to work this very loose batter for another 5 minutes. This is hard work but remember the reward is hot fried doughnuts!

- Once kneaded, cover with clingfilm or a clean tea towel and allow to rise for an hour in a warm draught-free place.

- Tip the risen dough out onto a floured surface and pat out. Roll to a thickness of about 1cm and cut out. In homage to Homer Simpson, that great consumer of doughnuts, I use a pint glass to cut out my doughnuts.

- Leave to rise again for a further 30 minutes. Heat 1.5cm depth of vegetable oil in a deep saucepan. Fry the doughnuts on one side until golden, flip over and fry on the other side. They will puff up as they fry. Drain on kitchen paper.

- Combine together the caster sugar and cinnamon. Toss the hot doughnuts in the cinnamon dust. Allow to cool slightly before filling with the apple.

- Take a piping bag and attach a plain tip, fill the bag with the remaining sauce. There are no gentle ways to do this. Stab the doughnut with the plain tip and inject a squeeze of apple sauce. Repeat with all the doughnuts.

- Consume the doughnuts without licking your lips – I bet you can't.

Shopping list

500g rhubarb

1 red onion

500g new potatoes

50g chorizo

2 fresh mackerel or 2 portions of smoked mackerel

From the storecupboard

Bicarbonate of soda

Butter

Eggs

Flour - plain and selfraising

Ginger - ground

Golden syrup

Oil - olive

Sugar - caster and demerara

Wine vinegar - red

Ginger snaps chain

Of all the spices and flavours in the world, ginger is one of the most evocative. It instantly conjures up thoughts of warm evenings inside as autumn turns to winter. That doesn't mean, of course, that you should restrict this chain to the colder, darker times of the year. In Britain at the moment that can mean the middle of August too!

Ginger snaps → use some of the ginger snaps to top a →
Rhubarb crumble → keep a small portion of the rhubarb before it goes into the crumble and make a salsa for →
Mackerel with rhubarb salsa → use some of the potatoes served alongside for →
Chorizo hash

Ginger snaps

My Mum was nothing if not predictable. Given a free rein along any supermarket biscuit aisle, you could bet she would return to the trolley clutching a packet of ginger biscuits. Ginger nuts, ginger creams, chocolate covered ginger snaps, brandy snaps – every variety imaginable. This is her recipe and making it transports me back into a kitchen where I would hang about on the off chance I might get to lick out a bowl.

Makes 24 biscuits

55g butter or margarine
30g caster sugar
110g golden syrup
110g self-raising flour
2 tsp ground ginger
½ level tsp bicarbonate of soda

○ Preheat the oven to 180°C/gas 4 and line two baking sheets with parchment.

○ Weigh out all your ingredients before you begin: I often don't and in this recipe you really must!

○ Put the margarine, sugar and syrup into a large saucepan and melt together over a low heat.

○ Sift the dry ingredients into a bowl.

○ Once the ingredients in the pan have melted, shoot the dry ingredients in and beat together with a wooden spoon. Make sure there are no lumps.

○ Allow to sit for a minute as the bicarbonate of soda needs to work and make the biscuit dough puff up.

○ Place heaped teaspoons of the mixture onto the baking trays. The dough will spread so make sure you leave space between them. Bake for 10 minutes until golden and crisp.

○ Cool for a minute or so on the tray and then transfer to a wire rack.

○ Time for a cup of tea and several magazines, I think.

Save it You'll need some biscuits for your crumble tomorrow.

Cook's tip Much as I love ginger, I do realise others of you may not. These snaps can be made with lemon zest to provide the zing we all love without the heat. Make the recipe in exactly the same way, but substitute 2 tsp lemon zest for the 2 tsp ground ginger. I find it best for this recipe to use a fine grater to zest the lemon rather than a zester that gives long shards of peel. Lemon snaps will also work well in the crumble topping, so the chain won't be affected whichever version you prefer.

Rhubarb crumble

Rhubarb crumble is without doubt one of the puddings that put the Great into Great Britain. Warming, comforting and with a hint of acid sharpness, this description could easily fit the many family members I watched making rhubarb crumble in my youth. Each took a simple recipe and made it their own. Some added oats to the topping for extra crunch, some rasped orange zest onto the rhubarb before it was cooked, and others added a zing to the dish with ginger. My version of rhubarb crumble uses some of the ginger snaps to add crunch and fire to this very familiar dish.

Serves 4

For the rhubarb filling
500g rhubarb, cut into 2cm lengths
100g caster sugar

For the crumble topping
50g ginger snap biscuits
250g plain flour
125g butter or margarine
125g demerara sugar

To serve
Custard, ice cream or cold pouring cream

○ Preheat the oven to 200°C/gas 6.

○ Place 400g of the rhubarb in the bottom of a deep baking dish. Place the remaining 100g rhubarb into a smaller separate dish for the salsa.

○ Add the caster sugar to the rhubarb for the crumble dish and mix well.

○ Pop the ginger snap biscuits into a bowl and, using the end of a rolling pin or your hands if you need a work out, crush the biscuits into crumbs. Add the flour, butter and demerara sugar and rub together with your fingers until the mix resembles breadcrumbs.

○ Spoon the crumble mixture over the rhubarb and bake for 30 minutes until the fruit is bubbling away through the topping.

○ At the same time, add a tablespoon of water to the smaller portion of rhubarb. Cover the smaller dish tightly with foil and bake for 30 minutes or until the rhubarb is softened.

Save it *Save the smaller dish for the salsa.*

○ Leave the rhubarb crumble to stand for a few minutes. Hot rhubarb crumble can resemble a lava field in both looks and internal temperature. Serve with custard, ice cream or very cold pouring cream.

Mackerel with rhubarb salsa

I really wish I wanted to cook and eat fish more than I do. Given that I am a complete gastronomic dustbin, for some reason I often forget about fish. Rhubarb salsa is so delicious and so addictive that I think I may have found a reason to pop some fish on my shopping list with far more regularity. Easy and quick to make and very versatile, rhubarb salsa works both with baked fish and also cold chunks of smoked mackerel. In either case, a steaming bowl of buttery new potatoes is the ideal accompaniment to this meal.

Serves 2

For the rhubarb salsa
1 red onion, finely chopped
1 tsp caster sugar
A pinch of salt
2 tsp red wine vinegar
100g roasted rhubarb
Freshly ground black pepper

For the fish and potatoes
2 fresh mackerel or 2 portions smoked mackerel
500g new potatoes
A knob of butter

To serve
Green vegetables

Make the salsa

○ Put 1 tbsp of the onion, sugar, salt and red wine vinegar in a small bowl.

Save it *Put the rest of the onion in an airtight container and keep for tomorrow.*

○ Using the back of a fork, break up the pieces of roasted rhubarb – you are looking for a lumpy mash rather than a smooth paste. Slide the rhubarb into the small bowl containing the onions and gently combine together.

○ Taste and add more salt or sugar if you think you need it. You are eating this, not me, so season for your palate. Leave to one side to cook the fish, if you need to, and boil the potatoes.

Bake the fish

○ Preheat the oven to 200°C/gas 6 and oil a baking dish.

○ Wash the fish inside and out, and season with salt and fresh black pepper. Lay the fish in the dish and bake for 20 minutes.

○ Whilst the fish is baking, boil the new potatoes in salted water. When cooked, drain, add the knob of butter and crush lightly with either a masher or a fork.

Save it *Put one-third of the cooked potatoes to one side for the last link in the chain. If you don't want to make the last link you can leave this portion uncooked or if you feel hungry just have a few more spuds with the mackerel dish – I'm not checking up on you!*

○ Serve the crushed buttery potatoes with the mackerel and a good spoon of the rhubarb salsa. If you need some greenery, a handful of ice cold peppery watercress would be my choice.

Chorizo hash

Rhubarb and ginger are both punchy flavours. Chorizo hash is no slouch in the taste department either. It doesn't matter much if you have the cooking chorizo or the sliced ready-to-eat version. The texture of the dish will be a little different but overall the finished dish will be about the same. Buy whichever you are going to use up.

Serves 2

1 tbsp olive oil
1 tbsp finely chopped onion (you should have some left from yesterday)
50g sliced or cooking chorizo, cut into small pieces
150g cold buttered crushed potatoes
1 egg
Salt and freshly ground black pepper

To serve
Chilli sauce or ketchup

○ Take a large frying pan and add a tablespoon of olive oil. Toss in the onion and cook until softened. Once the onion starts to soften, tip in the chorizo and cook until the oil begins to seep out and colour the onion.

○ Add the cooked crushed potatoes, stir into the chorizo onion mix and push to one side of the pan. Leave without stirring as you want the hash to get a crispy, crunchy bottom.

○ Tip the pan and encourage the oil from the chorizo to gather on the clear side of the pan. This is where you want to fry the egg. If you need a little more oil add some now.

○ Fry the egg to your liking: barely cooked, sunny side up, over easy – you choose. Drain the egg on some kitchen paper.

○ Slide the hash onto a plate, top with the egg and devour. Ketchup might be your condiment of choice but I'd go for chilli sauce here and really ramp up the zing.

Shopping list

4 cooking apples, such as Bramleys

450ml double cream

250g digestive biscuits

From the storecupboard

Bicarbonate of soda

Butter

Chocolate – dark

Cinnamon – ground

Cocoa powder

Cornflour

Eggs

Flour – plain

Gelatine, powdered

Glucose, liquid

Golden syrup

Milk

Oil – vegetable

Sugar – caster, granulated and icing

Vanilla pod or extract

Apple pie chain

This chain is definitely all about a little of what you fancy doing you good. For those days when you really could do with raising spirits all round, this apple pie chain could be just the ticket.

The keynote flavour is vanilla and custard.

Smooth and creamy textures link the apple pie chain together, from custard to ice cream, through hot chocolate and marshmallows, there is layer upon layer of the soft and silky to indulge.

Apple pie and custard → use the custard to make →
Honeycomb ice cream with chocolate sauce → use the chocolate sauce to make →
Hot chocolate and marshmallows → use the marshmallows and honeycomb to make →
Rocky Road

Apple pie and custard

Apple pie and custard has to be the culinary equivalent of a hug. Warming the kitchen as it cooks, filling the house with the aroma of apple and cinnamon, and getting everyone together in expectation of a fight for the skin off the custard!

Serves 4

For the pastry
250g plain flour, plus extra for dusting
125g butter or margarine
3–5 tbsp cold water
A little milk, to glaze

For the apple filling
3–4 large cooking apples, such as Bramleys
2 tbsp water
A knob of butter
1 tsp ground cinnamon
1–2 tbsp caster sugar

For the custard
300ml full-cream milk
300ml double cream
3 large egg yolks
1 tbsp caster sugar
1 tsp vanilla powder or extract or 1 vanilla pod

Make the pie
○ Preheat the oven to 200°C/gas 6 and grease a 20cm pie dish.

> **Save it** *Keep the egg whites or freeze them individually and then make marshmallow (page 188) or meringues (page 98).*

○ Place the flour and fat in a large bowl and rub in the fat until the mixture resembles breadcrumbs. Using a round-bladed knife, stir in the cold water a little at a time until the mixture begins to come together. Use your hands to form a ball of pastry. Wrap the pastry in clingfilm and leave it to rest for half an hour or so in the fridge.

○ Roll out half the pastry on a lightly floured surface and use to line the pie dish. Either prick the base with a fork or cover with baking parchment and fill with baking beans and bake in the oven for 15 minutes. Remove the paper and beans, if using, and allow to cool.

○ Meanwhile, peel and core the apples, then cut into generous-sized chunks. Place in a saucepan with a splash of water, a knob of butter, the cinnamon and sugar to taste.

○ Bring to a simmer, then gently cook the apple until the edges of each piece just begin to soften. Don't cook to a mush as the apple will continue to cook in the oven. Spoon the part-cooked apple into the part-baked shell, taste and sprinkle with a little more sugar if it tastes very sharp.

○ Roll out the remaining pastry into a circle and pop over the apple. Press together to seal the edges, then trim. Brush the top with milk and make a small slit in the pie crust to let steam escape. Bake for 20–30 minutes or until the pastry is golden brown and the apple is bubbling.

Make the custard

○ Warm the milk and cream together but do not allow this to get too hot.

○ Whisk together the egg yolks, sugar and vanilla powder or extract. If you are using a vanilla pod, split the pod, scrape out the seeds and whisk these into the egg and sugar mixture.

○ Pour the warm milk and cream mixture over the eggs and sugar, whisking all the time until well combined.

○ Return the mixture to the saucepan and slowly bring to a simmer, stirring continuously with a wooden spoon until the mixture thickens. Do not rush this or you will end up with sweetened scrambled eggs.

○ Place half the custard into a lidded container and keep for the ice cream recipe.

○ Serve the remaining thick, creamy custard poured all over a wedge of your apple pie.

> **Save it** If you are going to make custard regularly, you'll find that making vanilla sugar is more economical than buying lots of vanilla pods. Take a large-screw topped jar, pop in a vanilla pod, then fill with caster sugar. Place the lid on the jar and leave for a week. The vanilla flavour will infuse the sugar. Refill the jar as you go and you will have a lovely vanilla-flavoured sugar for custards and cakes. It's even more economical if you put one or two pods from which you have scraped the seeds for another recipe.

Honeycomb ice cream with hot chocolate sauce

Think of honeycomb ice cream and hot chocolate sauce as a Crunchie bar after a Gok Wan makeover: the same basic ingredients but put together with much more style and pizzazz. I am a huge fan of the freezing cold and boiling hot sensory combination. Something as simple as a really good *affogato* will satisfy my cravings but for those times when only chocolate will do, this is the recipe.

Serves 4

For the honeycomb
100g caster sugar
3 tbsp golden syrup
1 tsp bicarbonate of soda

For the ice cream
300ml cold custard
150ml double cream
1 tsp vanilla powder or extract

Hot chocolate sauce
300ml double cream
1 tbsp golden syrup
50g dark chocolate, grated

Make the honeycomb
○ Grease and base line a 20cm square tin.

○ Place the sugar and syrup in a deep, heavy-based pan over a low heat. Don't stir the mixture but gently swirl the pan to combine the two ingredients. Continue to heat together until the syrup and sugar mixture reaches the hard crack stage. That's 150°C on a sugar thermometer, or when ½ tsp of the syrup dropped into cold water crackles and spreads.

○ Remove the pan from the heat and tip in the bicarbonate of soda. The mixture will puff up like a volcano. Using a long-handled spoon, stir and pour the hot, foaming toffee into the prepared tin. Allow to cool.

Make the ice cream

○ Stir together the custard and the double cream. Churn in an ice cream maker until frozen, or pour the mixture into a shallow container, place in the freezer and stir every hour until set.

○ Break half the honeycomb into small pieces, stir into the mixture and freeze until hard.

Save it *Keep the remaining half of the honeycomb to use in the Rocky road recipe.*

○ When ready to serve the ice cream, remove from the freezer and allow to soften as you make the hot chocolate sauce.

Make the hot chocolate sauce

○ Put the cream, syrup and chocolate in a small pan over a low heat. Warm together until the ingredients are combined, stirring occasionally.

Save it *Keep the remaining chocolate sauce for your mug of hot chocolate later in the week.*

To serve

○ Take a couple of scoops of honeycomb ice cream and anoint with a generous spoonful of the sauce. Find a quiet place on your own and enjoy.

Hot chocolate and marshmallows

I know that long walks in the cold winter air should be reward in themselves. Communing with nature, admiring the view and trying not to get the boots too muddy ought to be enough. As someone who likes her countryside with street lamps, the lure of a hot chocolate bedecked with marshmallows might just tempt me out into the unknown – or at least the local park.

Serves 1

For the marshmallows
1 tsp flavourless vegetable oil, for greasing
4 tbsp cornflour
4 tbsp icing sugar, sifted
400g granulated sugar
1 tbsp liquid glucose
300ml water
2 sachets or 2 tsp powdered gelatine
Boiling water
2 large egg whites

For the hot chocolate
1 mug full-cream milk
1 heaped tbsp chocolate sauce

Make the marshmallows
o Oil a 15 x 30cm gratin dish.

o Mix together the cornflour and icing sugar, then sprinkle over the prepared dish.

o Place the granulated sugar, glucose and 175ml of the water in a large heavy-based pan and slowly bring to the boil. Place a sugar thermometer into the syrup and heat until it reaches hard ball stage. That's 128°C, or when ½ tsp of syrup dropped into cold water forms a hard ball. This will take several minutes.

○ Whilst the syrup is heating, pour the remaining water into a cup. Sprinkle over the gelatine and allow to swell up (also known as sponging!). Pop the teacup into a deep bowl and pour boiled water into the bowl around (not in!) the cup. Leave to stand for a few minutes until the gelatine has returned to a liquid. You can give it a stir if you need to.

○ When the syrup reaches the correct temperature, take it off the heat and allow to cool slightly. Whisk in the liquid gelatine mixture a little at a time – it will foam up as you do this so take care – then pop to one side to cool a little. Don't leave it too long or the gelatine will start to set.

○ Whisk the egg whites until they form soft peaks when you lift out the whisk. Continue to whisk but gradually begin to pour in the syrup a little at a time, continuing until all the syrup has been added. Keep on whisking until the whole confection is stiff and thick. You need a pour-able mixture that leaves a thick ribbon-like trail.

○ Scrape the foam into the prepared dish and set aside to cool. Overnight is good but lack of will power on my part makes this difficult.

○ Cut into squares and toss in the icing sugar/cornflour mixture still in the dish.

> **Save it** Use a few for your hot chocolate and reserve the remainder for Rocky road.

Make the hot chocolate
○ Heat together the mug of milk and a good heaped spoonful of the chocolate sauce. If you used the sauce up yesterday, a few squares of chocolate will do a similar job.

○ Top with several squares of marshmallow. You may like to snip these into smaller pieces if you want them to melt into your chocolate as you drink it.

Rocky road

As we all know which foods we should be consuming if we want to live long and healthy lives, we equally know when a particular item of food is definitely sinful. Rocky road is about as bad as it gets, and boy is it good! It may shorten my life by a day or so but, what the heck. Life is for living.

Makes 20 bars

250g shortcake or digestive biscuits
A handful of honeycomb, if you haven't eaten it already
A handful of marshmallows, snipped into small pieces
125g butter or margarine
1 tbsp cocoa powder
1 tbsp golden syrup
200g chocolate, milk or dark, as you prefer

○ Grease a 15cm square tin.

○ In a mixing bowl, using the end of a rolling pin, crush the biscuits into crumbs. Or put them in a double plastic bag (one inside the other) and crush with a rolling pin or a spoon. You could use a food processor but that takes all the fun out of it.

○ Stir in the honeycomb and marshmallows.

○ In a large saucepan, melt the butter, cocoa and syrup together, stirring until blended.

○ Pour into the bowl and stir everything together thoroughly. Tip the chocolaty rubble into a prepared tin and press down. Put into the fridge to set.

○ Once set, melt the chocolate in a heatproof bowl set over a pan of gently simmering water. Pour over the biscuit base. Refrigerate once more until the chocolate is set.

○ Cut into wedges and serve. This is best served from the fridge as it is only the fact that the ingredients are cold that holds it together.

Pimp it up *The sheer chocolate-ness of this cries out for the addition of some fruit. I like to add snipped up ready-to-eat dried apricots to the biscuit base when I'm using dark chocolate, or cranberries with a white chocolate topping. Add whatever you fancy. Made with ginger biscuits and dark, dark chocolate, this is a very adult treat. Sorry children!*

Shopping list

1 eating apple, such as Cox's

350g blackberries

1 pack samosa wrappers or filo pastry

300ml single cream

300ml double cream

1 tub ice cream

150g sweet snacks

100g savoury snacks

1l gin

From the storecupboard

Bicarbonate of soda

Butter

Cake sprinkles - hundreds and thousands etc.

Cardamom pods

Eggs

Flour - plain

Oil - vegetable

Sugar - caster, granulated and soft light brown

Blackberry gin chain

If I asked many people if they'd consider foraging for food I know I'd get a mixed response. Then I remind them that they almost certainly have done so in the past. Blackberrying! Armed only with an ice cream tub for collecting our treasures and a walking stick to pull down the out-of-reach branches that always held the most luscious berries, many a summer afternoon was spent picking and surreptitiously eating the blackberries. Pie or crumble was my Mum's destination of choice for our blackberries. Had she known about blackberry gin, however, it might have been a different matter altogether.

Blackberries run through the dishes in this chain like a ripple in a scoop of ice cream. Sweetened with sugar and sozzled with alcohol, the berries let their juices flow freely. The cardamom ice cream softens the acidity somewhat, with the biscuits providing a surprising bite.

Blackberry gin and nibbles → use the steeped blackberries to make →
Blackberry and apple samosas with cardamom ice cream →
Blackberry gin and nibbles → use the nibbles to make →
Really! biscuits → use the Really! biscuits and cardamom ice cream to make →
Ice cream sandwiches

Blackberry gin and nibbles

As this blackberry gin matures around the holiday season, it would be a crime not to make a blackberry kir royale. Fill a champagne flute a sixth full with the blackberry gin, top up with something fizzy, sit back and sip slowly.

Serves 4

350g blackberries, washed
350g granulated sugar
1l supermarket gin

- Put a 2l jar though the dishwasher, or sterilise in the oven. Allow to cool slightly.

- Tip in the washed berries and the sugar. Top up with gin. Screw on the lid. Invert the jar several times until the ingredients are well combined. Place in a cool dark cupboard. My jars sit next to the cereals!

- Daily for the next two weeks invert the jars a couple of times. The sugar will become syrup and the colour of the gin will darken.

- After a couple of weeks, continue to invert the jar every couple of days for another fortnight.

- Take a shot glass, pour a good slug of the blackberry gin, open a pack of your favourite nibbles, sit back and relaaaxxx.

○ Once a month is up, strain the berries from the liquid. You can now decant the liquid into a bottle of your choice. Beautiful bottles are available in many kitchen suppliers but I have resorted to a clean screw-topped wine bottle in the past.

○ Keep the berries to one side and use within a day.

○ Leave the gin to mature; I find that three months is a goodly amount of time. This gets you towards Christmas if you started in July or August.

○ You can also make this very easily from frozen berries at any time in the year but personally I find it tastes even better if you have picked the berries yourself.

Cook's tip *Why not try a variation of a Bramble? Two parts of blackberry gin to 1 part lemon juice. Shake over ice, strain and pour over a glass filled with crushed ice. If you still have a couple of sozzled blackberries, add them to the glass as a garnish.*

Blackberry and apple samosas with cardamom ice cream

These gin infused blackberries cry out to be used and not discarded. If you don't want to fuss with the samosas simply warm up the berries and pour over the cold, cold ice cream.

For the samosas
350g gin-soaked blackberries (you can use sober ones if you don't have sozzled berries)
1 eating apple, such as a Cox's, peeled and chopped
1 tbsp soft light brown sugar
1 pack samosa wrappers or filo papers
Vegetable oil, for shallow-frying

For cardamom ice cream
8 cardamom pods
300ml single cream
4 egg yolks
115g caster sugar
50ml gin
300ml double cream

Make the samosas
○ Combine the blackberries, apple and sugar in a large bowl.

○ Take a samosa wrapper and place 1 dessertspoon of the mixture at one end of the pastry. Fold the corner up to make a triangle, then continue this along the wrapper until all the pastry is used. Seal the end with a dab of water. Carry on this process until all the filling has been used.

Save it *You can now open freeze any samosas you may not need to keep for a later date. Once frozen, keep in a box or freezer bag in the freezer. Defrost thoroughly before continuing the cooking process or there will be lots of spitting, spluttering and a big mess.*

○ Heat the oil in a frying pan until moderately hot. Fry the samosas gently until golden brown and crisp. Drain on kitchen paper, arrange artfully on a plate, dust with icing sugar, if you must, and add a dollop of ice cream. Demolish with gusto!

Make the cardamom ice cream

○ Bruise the cardamom pods by crushing gently with the flat of a knife or the heel of your hand and pop into a saucepan. Pour over the single cream and bring slowly to scalding point. The cream will just begin to bubble around the edge of the pan. Remove from the pan and cool for 30 minutes or so. Strain the cardamom pods from the cream.

○ Whisk together the egg yolks and sugar until pale and foamy. Add the slightly cooled cream to the eggy mixture, stirring all the time. When combined, strain through a sieve back into the saucepan. Over a very gentle heat, keep the custard moving using a wooden spoon. Continue until the custard thickens. Remove from the heat. Add the alcohol and stir again. Cool and then refrigerate until ready to complete the next stage – at least 1 hour and up to 12 hours.

○ Whisk the double cream until it forms soft peaks. Using a spatula, fold in the cooled custard. Either churn using an ice cream machine until set or pour into a large plastic container and freeze for 1 hour. Whisk up with a fork and re-freeze. Continue like this until the ice cream is set. This may take up to 3 hours.

○ Serve a scoop of cardamom ice cream over the top of the warm blackberry samosas. Don't drive the car after this pudding it contains a great deal of gin.

Save it *Place any remaining ice cream back in the freezer ready for the ice cream sandwiches later in the week.*

Really! biscuits

The upshot of a slightly boozy evening is often several half bags of snacks lurking around the following morning. If my Mum were here the bags of nibbles would be decanted into little plastic pots or have their tops screwed shut and clipped tight with a brightly coloured plastic gizmo. I am not that organised so the snack detritus lays about daring me to eat it before it all goes soggy. But here is my cunning plan. I hide the snacks inside cookies. They are a great way to use up nibbles. Tasty and chewy, salty and sweet, Really! biscuits are an ideal adult cookie.

Makes 12–18 biscuits

150g sweet snacks (a mix of raisins, dried fruits, chocolate chunks, pieces of fudge, Maltesers, chocolate peanuts, Smarties, you get the idea!)
100g savoury snacks (salted nuts, popcorn, potato sticks, ready salted crisps, salted pretzels, plain Pringles, whatever is open – mind you, maybe not the wasabi peas!)
125g butter, softened
150g soft brown muscovado sugar
1 egg
150g plain flour
½ tsp bicarbonate of soda

○ Heat the oven to 180°C/gas 4 and line two baking trays with baking parchment.

○ Break the snacks into small pieces of about equal size.

○ Beat together the butter and the sugar. When well combined, add the egg and whisk again. Fold in the flour and bicarbonate of soda. Stir in the snacks and make sure they are well distributed in the mixture.

○ Take a dessertspoon of the mixture and roll it into a ball. Place it on the baking tray, leaving space between the spoons of mixture as they will spread as they cook.

○ Bake in the oven for 12–15 minutes.

○ Allow to cool on the tray slightly, then transfer to a cooling rack to finish.

Save it *No faffing around with twist ties and plastic boxes. Just pop any uneaten cookies in a tin for tomorrow.*

Ice cream sandwiches

Hardly a recipe, this is much more an assembly of parts already to hand. Ice cream sandwiches make the most delicious dessert at a barbecue – but be careful as they can be a little treacherous. If you are too eager to make them and don't let the biscuits cool enough, the ice cream will melt all over your best party frock. Leave it too long and the hard biscuit will compress the ice cream and send it squirting over the boss's wife!

Makes 1

2 Really! biscuits
1 scoop of ice cream
Vermicelli, hundreds and thousands, chopped nuts, decoration of your choice

○ Take a warm, but not too hot, biscuit. Place a scoop of ice cream onto the biscuit.

○ Top the ice cream with a second biscuit and press together slightly: remember the treachery I mentioned earlier and take care.

○ Roll the ice cream edges of the sandwich in a topping if you like. In my house this is compulsory; age is no barrier to this.

○ Eat and repeat until everyone is full.

Cook's tip *A quick and absolutely delicious dessert that uses up a spare scoop of ice cream is an affogato. As affogato is the Italian for 'drowned': you can see why as all you have to do is pour a shot of hot espresso over a scoop of cold ice cream. If you want a dinner party dessert version, you can add a slug of amaretto to the espresso before drowning your ice cream.*

Index

Some other Spring Hill/How To Books titles

EVERYDAY FAMILY FAVOURITES
Over 300 delicious wholesome recipes that you can easily cook at home

DIANA PEACOCK

'The only book you'll need to feed a growing family, whatever your budget.'

If you want your children to remember chocolate cakes and apple pies and freshly baked bread; bubbling hot steak and kidney pies with buttered mash; wonderfully light and healthy pasta; sherry trifles at Christmas and treacle toffee on Bonfire night; and lots of other homemade family favourites, then this is the book for you.

With over 300 clear and concise recipes for delicious, nutritious and heart warming food, here is a book that revives old fashioned, traditional home cooking using good, fresh, local ingredients.

It will show you how to make inexpensive recipes that ensure you eat well every day of the week. From light snacks to hearty main courses and home baking, you will discover how a cleverly stocked store-cupboard and simple recipes make tasty family meals whatever your budget. You can also use it to make your own bacon, sausages, pickles, baked beans, butter, yoghurt, cream and cheese.

Put your heart back into your cooking with delicious recipes that turn out as they are meant to. This book will show you how to prepare all the decent food a family will ever need.

ISBN 978-1-908974-00-6

THE LEFTOVERS HANDBOOK

An A–Z of every conceivable ingredient in your kitchen with inspirational ideas and recipes for using them

SUZY BOWLER

This books lists over 450 ingredients that you are likely to have left over in your cupboards, fridge or freezer and provides smart, interesting, sometimes quirky, but always delicious ways of using them up.

With this invaluable book in your kitchen you'll be able to get the utmost pleasure out of every scrap of food available whilst simultaneously being frugal. The waste it tackles is not simply that of money or of resources but of really good eating opportunities. The author also explains which flavours complement each ingredient and provides advice on how to store perishable items to prolong their freshness.

ISBN 978-1-908974-08-2

THE HEALTHY LIFESTYLE DIET COOKBOOK

SARAH FLOWER

Tired of fad diets and yo-yo dieting? Do you want to lose weight and improve your health but still enjoy your food? Nutritionist Sarah Flower believes that by following the recipes in her book you can eat well, lose weight, feel better AND stay that way. Sarah's focus is on healthy eating and delicious food that all the family will enjoy. She also describes lifestyle changes that everyone can adopt to lay the foundations for healthy eating and to lose unwanted pounds if they need to. Sarah also includes superfoods, menu plans and some food swap suggestions.

ISBN 978-1-905862-74-0

MAKING THE MOST OF YOUR PRESSURE COOKER
How to create delicious, healthy meals in double quick time

CAROLYN HUMPHRIES

This book will help you make the most of this invaluable and highly fuel-efficient kitchen appliance so that you can create really tasty meals in a fraction of the time of conventional methods.

Pressure cooking is simply the fastest, easiest, most economical way to cook healthy meals. You'll save money, time and energy. But that's not all: because pressure cooking keeps in so much more of the natural goodness content of foods, it's much healthier too. In *Making the Most of Your Pressure Cooker* you'll discover how to pressure cook complete meals, soups, desserts, vegetables and even preserves in double-quick time.

Carolyn Humphries has been a journalist and food writer for over 30 years. She has written for many women's, health and lifestyle magazines and is the author of over 60 books, including *How To Cook Your Favourite Takeaways* and *Everyday Curries*.

ISBN 978-1-908974-05-1

EAT WELL, SPEND LESS
The complete money-saving guide to everyday cooking

SARAH FLOWER

This invaluable book contains over 200 great family recipes for busy cooks who want to save time and money, but also deliver wholesome food for their families. It's also an essential housekeeper's guide for the 21st century. Nutritionist Sarah Flower shows you how to feed yourself and your family a healthy balanced diet without spending hours in the kitchen and a fortune in the supermarket.

ISBN 978-1-905862-83-2

EVERYDAY THAI COOKING
Easy, authentic recipes from Thailand to cook at home for friends and family

SIRIPAN AKVANICH

Everyday Thai Cooking brings you the secrets of cooking delicious Thai food straight from Thailand. Author Siripan Akvanich draws on her years of experience of cooking for her restaurant customers in Thailand to enable you to create authentic Thai dishes, ranging from curries and meat and fish dishes to wonderful Thai desserts. With clear instructions and insider tips, Siripan helps you bring these dishes – many of them traditional family recipes – to life and shows you how to make them *a-roi* (delicious)!

ISBN 978-1-905862-85-6

EVERYDAY COOKING FOR ONE
Imaginative, delicious and healthy recipes that make cooking for one fun

WENDY HOBSON

Here is a collection of simple, tasty meals – specially designed for one – that can help you enjoy your everyday eating. Starting with sensible tips for shopping and for stocking your food cupboard, you'll find recipes for everything from snacks to delicious fish; and meat and vegetable main courses that keep an eye on a healthy dietary balance – and a healthy bank balance. And there's a unique feature, too. Some recipes just don't work in small quantities, and that could include some of your favourites. So we've included some of those recipes – like casseroles, roasts and cakes – and shown you how to create four different meals from one single cooking session.

ISBN 978-1-905862-94-8